2016
THE BEST
MEN'S STAGE MONOLOGUES

2016
THE BEST
MEN'S STAGE MONOLOGUES

Edited by
Lawrence Harbison

SMITH AND KRAUS PUBLISHERS   2016

ISBN: 1-57525-907-9
ISBN: 978-1-57525-907-9
ISSN: 2329-2695

Typesetting and layout by Elizabeth Monteleone
Cover Design: Olivia Monteleone

A Smith and Kraus book
177 Lyme Road, Hanover, NH 03755
Editorial 603.643.6431 To Order 1.877.668.8680
www.smithandkraus.com

Printed in the United States of America

TABLE OF CONTENTS

Lawrence Harbison

Here you will find a rich and varied selection of monologues for men from plays which were produced and/or published in the 2015-2016 theatrical season. Many are for younger performers (teens through 30s) but there are also some excellent pieces for older guys as well. Some are comic (laughs), some are dramatic (generally, no laughs). Some are rather short, some are rather long. All represent the best in contemporary playwriting.

Several of the monologues are by playwrights whose work may be familiar to you, such as Don Nigro, Lee Blessing, Mark Roberts, Sam Bobrick, Wendy MacLeod, Richard Dresser and Deborah Zoe Laufer; others are by exciting up-and-comers such as Max Baker, Emily Schwend, C.S. Hanson, Abby Rosebrock, Chiara Atik and Merridith Allen.

Many of the plays from which these monologues have been culled have been published and, hence, are readily available either from the publisher/licensor or from a theatrical book store such as the Drama Book Shop in New York. A few plays may not be published for a while, in which case contact the author or his agent to request a copy of the entire text of the play which contains the monologue which suits your fancy. Information on publishers/rights holders may be found in the Rights & Permissions section in the back of this anthology.

Break a leg in that audition! Knock 'em dead in class!

Lawrence Harbison

Dramatic
Kurt, twenties

Kurt was in the SS before he was captured and sent to a prisoner of war camp in Minnesota. Here, he tells Franz, a new arrival to the camp, what he has learned about the Americans as he tries to recruit him as a spy.

KURT: You will have noticed the Negroes. They are used for menial tasks, such as stewards on trains. Many are actually soldiers, however. They fight and die for their country, but are not allowed to eat in restaurants. I have seen this myself: in a train station, in St. Louis, the Germans were escorted into a restaurant, under guard. We sat at tables and ate, while civilians watched us. The Negro soldiers were sent out, into the kitchen, and were not allowed to eat. Their enemies were treated better than their own soldiers. What do you suppose these Negroes thought when they saw this? You will have heard of lynching. This is a control method used by Americans, to keep the Negroes in place. Hundreds of them are hanged. For whistling at white women. For talking back. For making eye contact. This is why we will win the war. Americans are racists. You've got good blood, I can see that. Just by looking at you. We can still do our part, even as prisoners. I do not confide in every young man who arrives here. I select only a few, and even these must prove themselves. Your parents are both Aryans? It's clear, I see it. There are traitors among us. Right here. They chat with the enemy, they tell lies, they give away secrets. I need to know who they are. What they say. Where they go. The Reich needs you to do a great service. You are a prisoner, but you can still serve your nation. Don't answer now. There is time.

Think about your country. That's all I require now: think about your country.

Dramatic
Harvey, twenties

Harvey, a guard at a prisoner of war camp in Minnesota, has taken a German prisoner out for a beer. Here, he tells him why he's spending the war with this duty, instead of fighting the Germans in Europe.

HARVEY: It's my balance. Something about my inner ear. I stumble, can't always stay up straight. I fall asleep, I can't help it. I'm not lazy, I just fall asleep. They were going to put me in a tank crew, that's what my dad wanted. But the damn balance test. I was 4-F, working in a hospital, mopping the floor. My mom wouldn't talk to me. We're three generations military in my family. Great grandfather fought against Lincoln. We're proud. So when I flunked out, it was, well, bad. Like I'm not a man. Like I'm not even in this family. Dad pulled some strings, got me reclassified. But they wouldn't let me fight. Wouldn't let me on the ship. This is the best I could do. God damn baby sitter. *(Pause)* I know what you think about us. I'm not dumb, I see it. Stupid Yanks. Dumb farmer boys. No education, no culture. And you, with your music and your opera and your languages. Philosophy lessons in the camp. How could you lose the war? You're the master race. Your blood is pure. You don't have balance problems! Every last one of you is a son of a bitch. You're all cocky mother fuckers, you know that? Nazi bastards. You know something? If I hadn't invited you out, I'd kick your ass back to the Fatherland. You're damn lucky my ear is screwy, cause otherwise I'd be burning your villages down. And don't you forget it! I'll show you right now. I'll show you how a Yankee boy fights!

Seriocomic
Roman, twenty-six

Roman is a very quick-thinker, smart, talkative, energetic, lacking in social skills, driven to find meaning in life. Works at Trader Joe's. Roman is talking to his work-colleague and best friend Else, having discovered his Quest.

ROMAN: If I die on the side of a mountain, and my life flashes before my eyes, I know the one thing I'm not going to be thinking about is 'What more could I have done to satisfy baconless customers?' So the question is: which mountain am I going to climb, you know? I'm talking mountains. Like big—huge—colossal mountains. So—you know I have parentage, or lineage of the Russian persuasion—of the old Ruskies, the old vodka-drinkers so I did the clearest most simple google search possible and—like—what's the highest peak in Russia? Mount Elbrus. 18,513 ft high. Highest point in all of Europe which is fucking cool. You know what's really cool I found out about Mount Elbrus? Mount Elbrus is where Zeus chained Prometheus - for giving fire and arts and knowledge and shit to man - and Zeus was like all pissed off at him coz he thought man shouldn't have that kind of awareness you know, man should just be fornicating or whatever, . . . so Zeus fucking chained Prometheus to Mount Elbrus for eternity, and every day this big ass vulture creature would come down and rip his body apart eat his liver and then it would grow back and the same thing would happen day after day after day —and—technically—if you believe the mythology—he should still be up there.

Dramatic
Roman, twenty-six

*Roman is a very quick-thinker, smart, talkative, ener-
getic, lacking in social skills, driven to find meaning
in life. Works at Trader Joe's. After cutting the top
of his finger off in a blender accident, thus ending
his mountain-climbing quest, Roman goes off his
meds. He is talking to his friends Else and Liv, as
they hang at Else's place, getting high.*

ROMAN: See - this is what I'm—This is the shit—you're
both so fucking PTC and you can't even see it. Programmed to Consume. Mentally bullied into accepting
the ethos of commercialism under the guise of freedom.
'I pledge Allegiance to the Flag of the United States of
America, and to the Republic for which it stands, one
Nation under God, indivisible, with liberty and justice
for all.' How old were you when you learned that shit?
How many times did they make you say it, over and over
and over again. The greatest country in the world. If you
can dream it you can do it. Two for the price of one. You
know what this country is the greatest at?: Child abuse,
School shootings, divorce rates, mental disorders, plastic
surgery, prison populations, health costs, energy use,
obesity . . . Obesity! The fact that All You Can Eat is a
good thing blows my mind. Programmed to Consume
and to hell with the consequences. The day you started
suckling on artificial breast milk was the day you got
into your college debt, The day you made an emotional
connection to some cheap plastic Chinese toy by cuddling
it at night was the day you jumped on the bandwagon
of gluten intolerance and an obsession with how many
Instagram followers you have. The whole system's been

filtered through your mushy little brain to believe you're Special, Gifted, Talented, Creative, Express Yourself Be The Best Version of Yourself You Can Be Inventive Spelling Creative Math 'There's Only One You' Well, guess what, there's millions of you. There's a whole generation of you. Half the population of this country is under 35. 18O million of us all told we're different and special and awesome and smart—we were told we were smart before we even learned anything, for walking upright for tying our shoelaces for the first time We were given trophies for just walking through the door. Encouraged at school - at school!—to talk about our feelings! Meanwhile I bet, I bet some guy with a Madonna mic showed up at your school one day and got you all excited about selling crappy little products from a magazine and the more you sold the more chance you'd have to win a yo-yo or get inside one of those money-grabbing wind machines. And you wanted to get inside that machine so bad - for selling as much cheap-ass useless shit as possible - well guess what: now you're in it! We had Sony Camcorders shoved in our baby face since the day we were born, The concept of Recording Our Lives is more important than the Concept of living it. We weren't taught the world is our oyster We were taught the world is our audience. You think you're the star of your own TV show, but you're doing the same as everyone else: Buying more shit. More apps, more clothes, more coffee, more music, more websites, more channels, more celebrities, more outrage, better skin, faster travel, softer pillows, things you should eat, things you shouldn't eat, ten places to visit before you die, fifteen warning signs of brain cancer, more clicks, more downloads, more Likes more swipes, more friends all thinking the same thing. None of this ever occurred to you before? We're experiments of commerce. but you confuse the word More with the word Choice. You think Desire means Deserve. You've got FOMO because everyone else has it. Now we're fucking holding it in our hands. We carry this shit around with us - input upon input upon input with shorter and shorter time to assess whether that input has any value. When will it end? How much can we consume before we figure out how worthless all this shit is?

Dramatic
Adam, fifty

In Breach, a young psychotherapist inherits three of her mentor's patients—one of whom may have been his murderer. The mentor, Dr. Adam Ferris, is giving his protégé a pep talk, as his grandiosity begins to spin out of control.

ADAM: I'm going on TV. You know that chef who fixes restaurants? Same format. I'll be visiting a bunch of clinics. See, you don't know this about me: back East I worked with a lot of chronic patients. I'd go into a teaching hospital, ask them to trot out their most intractable case, some hopeless catatonic who hadn't blinked for twenty-five years—whose eyeballs they had to irrigate so they wouldn't dry out—and within five minutes we'd be chatting away like old friends. This one silent old woman, I'll never forget, she used to line up all her vegetables on the plate so neatly she couldn't bring herself to eat them. So I sit down next to her, I reach over, and I mess up her nice row of peas. Right away she starts screaming. Lodges a complaint. Accuses me of sexual harassment. She was talking for the first time in years, but that irony was lost on the administration. Paranoids, too, I can usually make them come off it, the ones who think they're Jesus. "Gee, what a boring delusion. Can't you do better than that?" Or you play along with their fantasies, it creeps them out, they come off it. Romy's a prime example. But again, watch out. She's charming— her delusions are charming—but that can literally drive you crazy. (*pause*) It's getting harder to make ends meet. People come twice a month. The policies won't pay for anything more. They want instant results. They're like college students giving e-vals. Everything's user-friendly. It fucked up higher education and now it's fucking up psychotherapy. You could even piggyback onto my deal. They always need pretty women on TV. Not full time of course. Once I decided on this new direction? And cut the cord with Gloria? The weight of the world fell from my shoulders. For the first time in years I actually feel cheerful! And you know what they say—a completely cheerful man will live forever. So don't worry about me. Accept the challenges I'm giving you, stay calm, stay vigilant, and don't get lost in the labyrinth. You're better than you think you are.

For information on this author, click on the WRITERS tab at www.smithandkraus.com.

Dramatic
Kevin, twenty-five

Kevin McFadden committed a mass shooting three weeks ago, and hasn't spoken to anyone since. In BROKEN, he agrees to talk to Dr. Palmer, a psychiatrist at the prison where he's staying, who seems to have an uncanny ability to relate to Kevin. During their encounter, Palmer is finally able to get Kevin to reveal what led him to commit this horrific act.
In this monologue, Kevin explains his lifelong struggles with dating, relationships, and feeling loved.

KEVIN: We knew each other growing up. We went to church together, sang in the choir.

(He smiles.)

She had this lisp - she always used to say "Amaything Graze." I loved that. *(pause)* She moved back home after college, and we just kind of started talking on Facebook, andthen . . . She was just, like, everything I had been waiting for . . . . She was really smart and pretty, we had like everything in common. And she was the first girl - the only girl - that I really liked that ever said yes.

(He gets lost in the memories of her.)

She did this thing with her face, she scrunched it up when she got really happy. The first time I kissed her, I just remember staring at her face . . . She had the biggest smile . . . I mean, I thought that was it. That all the pain, all those years had been for something. Even if everything else was crap - I still had her. We did everything together, we read all my stories . . . I loved her. *(Pause)* And then —just, like, out of the blue she started taking longer and longer to write back. And she was always busy. So finally

I asked her, and she said she didn't feel "it." It was such bullshit. I was like - we did all that stuff, there's no way you would have done that if you didn't feel "it." And she said she thought if she kept trying maybe she would feel that way, but she never did. And that was it. She just left. *(Pause)* I read this article about a guy who lost half his face in a car accident - his eyes, his nose. He just got married. How pathetic is that? A guy with no face can find someone, but I can't. ADD SPACE It's always the same. Every time. Every girl I've ever dated - they all said the exact same thing. They don't like me that way. They don't feel "it." How can I make them feel "it?" How can I make someone love me?

Lloyd Suh

Seriocomic
Monkey, Pan-Asian, any age (could be any gender)

The Monkey is to Frank Chan sorta as Harvey is to Elwood P. Dowd. Nobody can see him except for Frank. Frank has broken up with his girlfriend but he's hooked up with a chanteuse he met in a bar in Chinatown. They're in bed Doing It, while the Monkey talks to the audience.

MONKEY: Oh yeah, babies. That's what I'm talking about. Let's give them a little privacy while we set up for the next thing. But just to stay thematically pertinent while they're doin what they're doin, let's talk about love. What do I love about love? I love bodies jumbled together but I love souls jumbled together even more, slippin and slidin like noodles in a big big plate of chicken chow mein. You don't know where one of em ends and one of em begins, because in that big ol plate, them noodles is all just noodles together, dig? Swimming in a big ol sea of chicken and Chinese vegetables. In this way, it is just like being Chinese in America. See, we are urged to believe that it is irreconcilable to be Chinese and American. That in order to be truly American, one must assimilate and overcome the brutal barbarism of Chinese culture. One must not only lose the gross staccato accent but also eliminate from themselves all those vile indications of otherness. You gotta be just like the white man. And then you can go to a Chinese restaurant and order in English. And the Chinese storekeeper will look at you and say, "You Chinese?" and you will say "Nope". And she will think about it, hmm, "You Japanese?" and you say "Nope!", this time getting a little prouder of the "No", but now she's on a roll, "You not Korean!", and you both laugh at this absurdity, of course you are not Korean and to end the conversation and because your food is now ready (you ordered General Tso's), you tell her confidently: "I'm American". And the proud way you say it makes this Chinese storekeeper gleam with admiration. Wow, she will think, maybe one day I can be like this enlightened American. . . . And that's what it looks like to hate yourself.

Dramatic
Roy, fifty-five

Roy, a private detective on a Caribbean island, is investigating the disappearance of Peter and Jane's daughter. Here, he reveals to them why he became a detective on this particular island.

ROY: I'm on your case because I understand what you're going through. I got the same call you did. Fifteen years ago. Your daughter is missing. My wife and I came down here. Just like you. We went back home but I couldn't sit in an office any more. I lost my faith. All I had left was what I could do with my hands. Create something that wasn't there before. So I started doing random jobs for people. Building a deck, making furniture. I'd come down here trying to find Mandy and finally I just stayed. I kept seeing her, she was always across the street or going around a corner, my heart would start pounding and I'd rush to catch up to some girl who didn't look a bit like her. It came down to a choice, go crazy or try to do something good. Like stopping this stuff. So I became a cop. And you know what? After all these years I still see my daughter every day. *(Pause)* Mandy worked so hard in high school, National Honor Society, volleyball captain, she was already accepted at Washington U. The school trip came along and she was desperate to go. I was all for it, I never got a chance to do anything like that when I was young. It was just about the only argument with Karen I ever won. So it's my fault we lost her. The point being, I do understand. I understand you've got your doubts about me. I started working with the cops down here on my daughter's case. I found out I had a real talent so I stuck with it. I'll send over clippings of the cases I broke. The kids I saved. You'll see. The two of you need to take care of each other. The one thing I know is, you won't make it out alone.

Dramatic
Fletcher Driscoll, forty-eight

Fletcher is a theater director who has returned to his hometown/alma mater to direct a questionably timed production of Romeo & Juliet. Here, he makes his opening remarks to his cast at their first rehearsal. He has flair but is not flamboyant.

FLETCHER: Good afternoon, my name is Fletcher Driscoll. Some of you may know my work. Those of you who don't keep up with the Alumni Accomplishments section of the website, will not. As you all must be painfully aware, a year ago, there was a shooting on this campus. It was not your typical school shooting. The man who pulled the trigger . . . a young engineering student bearing the unexceptional moniker Glenn Adams. His motive . . . something as common as breathing air. Unrequited love. By all reports, Young Mister Adams discovered that his long-time girlfriend and fellow classmate Carolyn Richardson was going to leave him for their teaching assistant, a graduate student named Christopher Blake. Adams shot both of them before turning the gun on himself. Mr. Adams and Ms. Richardson did not survive, but the other victim, Mr. Blake, pulled through. Young love. Untimely death. Unexpected survival. What other play could this University's theater department possibly choose to commemorate the anniversary of this tragedy but *Romeo & Juliet*? Now, some people see nothing tactless, offensive or even troubling about staging a play that culminates in the brutal slaying-and-double-suicide of three fictional young people being used to commemorate the brutal attempted-murder-slash-murder-suicide that felled three actual young people just outside our theater doors. Many, many others disagree finding it at worst exploitative and at best, inappropriate. So here we are. You are all exceptional talents, which is why this ill-timed venture will be a model of great theater, indelible romance, and most importantly . . . miraculously good taste. Now I've done my share of crazy Shakespeare. Some of it's been rather successful. Some of it . . . was on stage and we'll leave it at that. Because of the delicate nature of this production, I've decided to go a more traditional route. Sorry to disappoint, but this year Verona will be set . . . in Verona. Italy. Will this play be the same-old standard *Romeo & Juliet*. God, I hope not! What will make it special? What risks will we take? That, my friends . . . is the mystery. Now . . . let's begin.

For information on this author, click on the WRITERS tab at www.smithandkraus.com.

Dramatic

Fletcher Driscoll, forty-eight

Fletcher has worked up the nerve to describe an incident from thirty years ago to his boyfriend Jeff, 52. Note: the dialogue in parenthesis is not meant to be spoken; it is only there to provide context for incomplete sentences.

FLETCHER: We were horsing around . . . Just the usual stuff at first—wrestling, punching. It was what we did. Not in the face or anywhere my parents would see. But this one day, things got a little . . . *(intimate)* I mean, he didn't kiss me or anything. He never did that. But we started messing around and he eventually he wanted me to . . . "use my mouth." I was fifteen, I had never done anything like that. But he pinned me down on the bed and . . . made it clear that I wasn't going anywhere until I did it. The funny thing is . . . I never actually came right out and said "No. I won't do that. Stop it." I told him I didn't want to but . . . that never mattered to him before, so . . . And then it happened. *(pause)* For years, I wondered if I actually wanted it to. But the more I thought about it, the more I realized: no, that's not why I didn't stop him. I didn't tell him "no" . . . because it never occurred to me that I could. Why would it? I had become so accustomed to not having a say in anything he did to me, that . . . (I didn't say anything that time either) *(beat)* About an hour later, my mom came and picked me up. I was terrified she'd be able to tell, but . . . of course, she couldn't. I was a wimpy fifteen-year-old theater fag with gangly arms, a spare tire, and bad skin. So when the big, strong, handsome older boy wanted to spend all his time with me, well . . . And I loved him. So much. Of course everything I loved about him was imaginary. I figured that out eventually. But at the time, I knew that "deep down he really cared about me." Stupid.

For information on this author, click on the WRITERS tab at www.smithandkraus.com.

Dramatic
Christopher Blake, late twenties-early thirties

Christopher survived an on-campus shooting a year ago. He thought he had stolen a girl (Carolyn) from her boyfriend (Glenn), but Glenn found out and shot all three of them. Glenn and Carolyn died. Tonight, the University is commemorating the shooting with a production of Romeo & Juliet. Christopher is unloading long-held secrets to the play's director, Fletcher Driscoll, at the intermission. They are standing at the exact spot where the shooting took place. Note: the dialogue in parenthesis is not meant to be spoken; it is only there to provide context for incomplete sentences.

CHRISTOPHER: I know people are upset that they're doing this play. Honestly, when I heard about it, I was like . . . why not just reenact the shooting? But watching it tonight, I realized . . . Romeo and Juliet each chose to take their own lives because they thought they couldn't be together. But Carolyn . . . She didn't have a choice, he just . . . (killed her) Of course, the one thing art and life have in common is . . . If Romeo had waited a few minutes, Juliet would have woken up and he would have gotten the girl. Glenn would have too. Everybody thinks Carolyn was leaving Glenn for me. Including Glenn, obviously. But the truth is . . . she had just dumped me. We had been hooking up for a while and it was starting to get serious. So, we decided she should end things with Glenn. In fact, when I saw her that day, I thought she had. But instead . . . She told me she couldn't do it. That when she woke up that morning, she realized she still loved Glenn and what she felt for me was . . . Infatuation. And she was sure that after we spent some time away from each other, I'd realize that's all it was too. I wanted her to be (right). I prayed for it and I am not a praying man. But every morning it felt more and more like I'd lost a limb.

(Laughs to himself.)

A limb that didn't need me. But I needed her. I still need her. So I get why Romeo and Juliet did what they did. I even get why Glenn did what he did. He thought Carolyn broke his heart, but she didn't. Glenn's heart-break was all on me. All of this is on me. I knew what I was doing. I knew Glenn was . . . fragile. He was one of those super-smart but super-awkward kids. Kids . . . He was twenty but he looked fifteen. You can tell he had it really hard growing up. And he knew how lucky he was to have her. So did I. When I was recovering in the hospital, I started to realize how much he had opened up to me. That he kind of looked up to me. All I saw him as was easy competition. God, I was such a dick. And their families . . . They didn't want to hear from me. To them I was the guy who couldn't keep it in his pants and got their kids killed. I get to walk around. And two people who deserved to live their lives with each other can't do that anymore. We already had Romeo and Juliet to tell us that. Nobody else had to suffer. Now that's tragic.

For information on this author, click on the WRITERS tab at www.smithandkraus.com.

Dramatic
Garrison, thirties-forties, any ethnicity

Garrison, an environmental lobbyist, is arguing with his partner (spouse) Nate about the possibility of taking a job in Cleveland.

GARRISON: You want an easy answer? There isn't one. It's ALL fucked. ALL of it. You're trying to make this about you, but you're not hearing me!!! One day I'm practically saving the rain forest, the next day I'm serving "late lunch" cocktails to whiny little D.O.S. hacks with bullshit recs and wet diapers. *Apple-fucking-tinis?* Are you kidding me????!!! Ten years of my life went down with that firm. Everything, everything I was fighting for. And now, I get up every day and want to blow my goddamn brains out, like anything I am makes a fucking bit of difference. You think I want to go to Cleveland?! Fuck Cleveland. It's all the same. Here, Cleveland, whereverthefuck, nothing *matters* anymore, don't you get that? We're disposable! A decent job, a good one . . . don't you remember when it meant something? It was *earned*. It was *kept*. It was that epic DNA shit, man, our fathers and grandfathers and everything they worked for, like their fucking souls, their fucking lives depended on it. All gone. The world we live in now . . . it's fucking Vegas. All flash – ALL IN - and then you lose, you fucking lose, and then you ride your sensibly-priced commuter bike home in the pouring down rain with a fucking pink slip stuffed down your throat. Appletinis? If I'm gonna to die for a job, Nate, I want it to matter.

Seriocomic,
Claude, fifty

*On a movie set in the early 1940s, the actors in The
Wolf Man, are having lunch. Maria, notorious for
having an obnoxious pet monkey, is playing the old
Gypsy woman, Bela, typecast usually as a vampire,
is playing her son, and Evelyn is the pretty ingenue.
Lon, who is playing the title character, had a famous
father with the same name, and is in despair because
he knows he doesn't have his father's talent, and
feels he will never measure up. He also has a serious
drinking and anger management problem. Claude is
a very accomplished stage actor and teacher who is
now making a living playing sophisticated villains in
Hollywood movies. Here Claude is trying to help Lon
gain the confidence to play his role and accept who
he is. Claude is smart, funny, kind, rather sad, and
burdened with his own acting liabilities, in his case
that he is very short and not handsome. He is trying
to teach Lon to accept and work within his limitations, both as an actor and a person. Larry Talbot is
the character Lon is playing, who turns into the Wolf
Man. Claude is playing his father. The reference to
Bela never drinking wine is from his Draculan past.
Claude played the Invisible Man in another movie.
All of the actors, exiles of one sort or another, are
very much aware that a terrible world war is on the
horizon.*

CLAUDE: Listen. This Larry Talbot fellow also has a powerful, impressive father. Myself, actually. And he's a
good person. He never wanted to hurt anybody. He begs
them to put him in a cell when the moon is full. That's

why you're going to be great in this role. You are the Wolf Man. You were bitten by your father, so to speak, and when the moon is full you turn into somebody else, somebody who has all this violence in him. You don't want to be like that. You fight it. And if we can see that, look into your eyes and see the pain of that, you will transform this ridiculous piece of superstition and Gothic Hollywood claptrap into something which, if not art, at least will be gripping and quite powerful and will pull them in and perhaps actually mean something to somebody. We're all stuck with what we've got. I'm short, Bela's got his Hungarian accent, Maria's got her monkey, Evelyn is young and innocent. We use what we have, in our lives and in our art. You wish you could be as brilliant as your father. Well, you can't. But you can be good in your own way, find your own truth. I wish to hell I was a foot taller and looked like Errol Flynn. Not going to happen. Nevertheless. Maria will be the Gypsy Woman. Bela will never drink wine, Evelyn will make us fall in love with her, I will be the Invisible Man, and we'll do the best we can to find what truth is there, and give that truth as a gift to all those poor unfortunate victims out there sitting in the dark who have no idea what actual horrors are about to descend upon them. This is the role you were cast in. Play it.

Dramatic
John, thirties, African American

John, a lawyer, I speaking to his wife, Siomara. He has just found out that his Siomara is pregnant and she might not want to have their baby. They had argued at home and Siomara had disappeared. John has found Siomara in her parent's house. He's been patient until now, but he lets loose here and tells her how he really feels. He really wants this baby, and he just can't understand why she doesn't.

JOHN: Your neck is sexy, Simmy. I like to touch your neck . . . For fuck's sake, this is the second time you say something like that. I'm like a fucking mouse and you make me out to be domestic abuser #1. What the hell is this about? I want to have a baby with you. You've always been so fucking selfish, you know that. You talk about everybody else, Simmy, everybody else draining you, taking things from you but that's all you've ever done to me. You've used me. It's my turn now. I want you to feed us. I want to watch you breast feed and I want to feed from you after. I want to suck from you, take milk from you. I want to drain you like you've drained me. Is that so wrong? I want this. I really want this baby. I want it more than I want straight teeth or nice suits or, I don't know, clean underwear. I want it more than good healthcare for America or a world without terrorism. Fuck the terrorists. I can stand terrorism as long as I have this baby. Do you get that? More than winning a case, more than being on top, more than being successful, or the apple of your god damn eye. I want dirt. I want our house to get dirty. Real, dirty love, Simmy. I feel like we signed a contract and you're not following through.

I feel and I feel this from the bottom of my heart. That you're . . . that you're being such a selfish, selfish . . . Yeah, that's right. I am going to say it. I'm gonna to say it. A bitch. Fuck you.

For information on this author, click on the WRITERS tab at www.smithandkraus.com.

Dramatic
Michael, late thirties-early forties

Michael's mistress, Nora, has been beaten unconscious by his wife and is in the hospital. Michael is sitting with her, playing an episode of Designing Women on his laptop.

MICHAEL: Man, those ladies are hilarious! Like, Suzanne and Julia, geez, I can never decide which one I like better . . . I mean maybe you don't even remember this, cause you were wasted, but. You once told me this was your dream in life. Just watching *Designing Women* with me and margaritas and Chipotle . . . This is probably not how you pictured it. It was sposed to be in a cabin, we were sposed to snuggle, can't really do those things right now. Margaritas seemed inappropriate. As did reading my poems, so I left those at home, but. There's definitely a couple in there about you . . . They didn't do a very good job, tying your hair back . . . Hey remember that time you threw my phone down the toilet?? Haha . . . That was um. Oh. That was cause I said I don't believe in heaven. Man, you were—that really um . . . I could tell it really hurt your feelings, that I didn't believe in God. All those treacherous conversations, miracles, Lazarus we talked about . . . Course we stopped having em, but. I love that you believe in him. I don't love that in most people but I love it in you. And I loved it in my wife, to be honest. You were both . . . so fearful, for my stupid soul . . . And I gotta say, if you survive this, I'll believe in God. If your body heals, and you can wake up, to happier life . . . I am actually praying for that. So desperately . . . It would be a joke, it'd be truly obscene, for me to sit here, and take your hand. And tell you I love you. Just being in the same room with you, I love . . . And how s . . . how sorry I . . . Ah, god. I did this to you myself.

Dramatic
Dostoyevsky, forties

The great Russian novelist Fyodor Dostoyevsky has one month to write a novel or he must give up the rights to his collected works. He's hired Anna, a young girl, to take dictation, to speed the process up. But he's a tortured soul, haunted by his arrest and near-execution for treason, his years in a prison camp in Siberia, and the characters and visions that crowd his head and trouble his sleep. Here, he is trying to explain to Anna how it felt to come so close to being executed, and why the images crowding in his head make it difficult for him to concentrate.)

DOSTOYEVSKY: Characters jabbering, landscapes, visions of alleys in cities, teeming with life like the creatures in a pond, so much I could not possibly have written it all down—the God of Creation flooding my head, bursting to get everything out before his destructive Other Self could murder me. Then they tell you tomorrow you're going to die. You wait all night, in a state of unspeakable dread, your mind racing, praying for a miracle, hoping it's all a dream, until you hear the birds beginning to stir. And you want them to shut up, because the birds bring the dawn. They sing and sing, more and more of them, making a terrible racket. And then somebody opens your cell and takes you down a long, damp corridor towards a courtyard. The death sentence is read out. We're set with our backs against posts, sobbing and gibbering, at the edge of extinction, terrified beyond imagining. There's a row of men with guns and in a moment these men are going to shoot you. Bullets will come tearing into your body. You imagine the agony, the blood. You wonder how long it will take to die. Will one of them come and shoot you in the head to finish you off? Will you lie there in a puddle of blood, begging for mercy, or will you just look at him? Will he look you in the eye when he puts the gun to your head and blows your brains out?

Dramatic
Isayev, forties

Arrested for treason, nearly executed, a convict in Siberia for four years, the great Russian novelist Dostoyevsky must spend the rest of his sentence in the military in a remote Siberian town, where he falls hopelessly in love with a beautiful but nervous and unhappy young woman who is married to Isayev, a large, intimidating man who is out of work and drinking heavily. Isayev can see that Dostoyevsky is in love with his wife, and does not, for the most part, consider him a serious rival. He enjoys confusing and intimidating Dostoyevsky, combining professed friendship and a grudging admiration with thinly veiled threats. Here Isayev's wife has just complained that he never washes, and Isayev responds by putting his arm around Dostoyevsky, who is very nervous, warning him to be careful how far he goes with his wife.

ISAYEV: Life is too short to waste performing the same pointless tasks over and over. Why wash when you're just going to get dirty again? The earth is made of dirt, and so are we. My wife is compulsively clean. She washes and washes constantly. I tell her, she's going to scrape her beautiful skin entirely off her body, but she never listens to me. I speak gibberish because people who speak the truth they kill or send to Siberia. And yet we've committed no crime. This one, however, has committed a crime. He had ideas. To have ideas is a very great crime in Russia. A good Russian has no ideas. Just vodka. If you feel an idea coming on, quick, more vodka. Ideas are what kill Russians. Also vodka, but with vodka, at least you die happy! Or at least stupid, which is much the same thing. Ideas only make people miserable. You are a man with too many ideas. You're going to be very, very miserable. And as if that weren't enough, you're in love with my wife, and that is the greatest catastrophe that could befall any man. I know whereof I speak. I am a bigger fool than you. I'm a man who's in love with his wife. There is no spectacle on earth more pitiful. And now I'm out of vodka. Life gets more and more tragic. I'm going out to look for work. But with any luck I won't find it. Take care of my wife while I'm gone. I can tell that you and I are going to be great friends. We will sit and drink together, and I'll tell you how beautiful my wife looks when she's naked, and you will be very, very miserable. And then you will go and write books about people who are miserable. And everybody who reads these books will be miserable. This is why art is so wonderful. But not as good as sexual intercourse.

Dramatic
Dostoyevsky, forties

*The great Russian novelist Dostoyevsky, trying des-
perately to finish a novel in a month or lose his entire
life's work to an unscrupulous publisher, has been
trying to explain his life to his young stenographer.
Here he attempts to describe his tortured creative
process, and how it seems intimately connected,
somehow, to his love for a series of very appealing
but extremely difficult women who make him utterly
miserable. The woman in question is a beautiful but
troubled person he met while serving out the military
part of his treason sentence. As he declares his love
for this woman, who is married to a rather
intimidating and dangerous drunkard, we can see
both what is so earnest and appealing about him and
also what makes women so uncomfortable. He loves
intensely but something in him seems to sabotage all
his efforts to connect.*

DOSTOYEVSKY: I myself am very stupid, the way a great
genius can be stupid. I wish I could make myself feel
real. I'm either not real at all or far too real to be sane.
I know the key is to remain calm, but I can't, because
0f the fire burning in my head, and that's how creation
occurs, as a kind of spontaneous combustion. It's this
burning and itching, and you want it to stop, but when
it stops, you die. Or if you don't die, you might as well
have. I have no talent for life, but how can I write when
life keeps presenting these obscene manifestations to
me, filling my brain with so many distractions, and so
many revolting smells? And being in love is the worst
thing of all. What incredible follies one commits under

the demented promptings of misguided lust. I can't help it. I've always had these premonitions. I think they're connected to the fits. Just before I met you, I found myself in a state of frenzied expectation that something was going to happen to me—that I'd grown ripe for something, maybe something terrible, but inevitable. And then I met you. And now you're all I can think about. All day I think about you, waiting for a chance to see you. Then I see you, and the time seems to rush by. I don't say what I wanted to say. I don't do what I wanted to do. And then it's over. And when I walk out the door I feel as if I've died. Then I lie there half the night staring at the ceiling in the dark and thinking about you. And then I fall asleep and dream about you. But just as I'm about to possess you, I wake up. And then I can't get back to sleep, and the picture of you being violated by your husband rises up in my head and I want to die.

Dramatic
Isayev, forties
Mid-nineteenth century

*The great Russian novelist Dostoyevsky, serving out
the remainder of his treason sentence in the military
in Siberia, has fallen in love with a beautiful but
troubled married woman who is making him very
miserable. Her husband Isayev is a large, intimidating drunkard who has for some time enjoyed tortur-
ing and threatening Dostoyevsky while   professing
friendship to him. His contempt for the lovesick
writer is tempered with jealousy and a bit of envy,
and in fact, Dostoyevsky might be his only friend.
Here Isayev, in the last stages of drinking himself
to death, is attempting to scare Dostoyevsky away
from his wife while at the same time recognizing
that after he dies they will very likely sleep together.
He loves his wife, but she drives him insane, and he
hates Dostoyevsky, but has a strange affection, even
respect for him, even as he's humiliating and terrify-
ing him.*

ISAYEV: I am drunk, and I'm also dying. Soon I'll be dead,
and other men will fuck my wife, which is to me an obscenity appalling beyond all imagining. And I can't stop
imagining it. Yet I know it's foolish to be disturbed by
such a thing. No man can ever really possess a woman he
loves. They are what kills us. Love kills us. Listen to me,
idiot. When I am dead, whatever you do, however much
you are tempted, do not fuck my wife, or I swear to you
I will claw my way out of my coffin and up through the
mud that covers my grave and crawl in your window at
night and suck out your brains through your ears. But if

you must fuck my wife, take care of her, and your reward will be that she kills you, too, and you'll deserve it for being stupid enough to love her, and for fucking a dead man's wife. We waste most of our lives evacuating our bowels and manufacturing shoe polish or carving toy weasels when all the while there is an unspeakable secret beauty concealed in everything, but the minute we reach out for it, it vanishes. Beauty is a terrible thing. An awful thing. Because it has not been fathomed. We will never get to the bottom of it. God sends us nothing but riddles, and we exist in the darkness where all the boundary lines meet, and all contradictions exist at the same time. It's terrible what mysteries there are. And before we can solve them, God comes like a gigantic bear and rips off our head and devours us. I pity you, my friend. You are going to live.

Dramatic
Tolstoy, fifty

The great Russian novelist Dostoyevsky, suffering from repeated epileptic attacks and harrowing nightmares, is having a vivid hallucinatory encounter at a train station with his rival Tolstoy, who is trying to decide whether or not his heroine, Anna Karenina, should throw herself under a train or sit down to a lobster dinner instead. Tolstoy and Dostoyevsky admire each other grudgingly but have very different views of the world, and a great deal of trouble understanding one another. Tolstoy is a realist, a moralist and a rationalist who feels an almost overpowering compulsion to write but has serious doubts about his profession. Dostoyevsky is a passionate and maniacal expressionist, whose people behave in contradictory, self-defeating and sometimes inexplicable ways. Here, Tolstoy tries to explain to Dostoyevsky why he disapproves of him, but also reveals his mixed feelings about his own role as the god of the fictional universes he creates.

TOLSTOY: You spend all your time reaching your dirty hands into the guts of the worst and rooting around to find pearls there. Although I must admit, you're good. Insane, but good. But all of this fuss. All of this pointless anguish. All this darkness in your soul. You tell yourself it's necessary for creation, but if that's really the case, then a person can do without creation. Peace in the soul and love for others. That's all that matters. That's what I tell myself, anyway. But in fact, my own soul is as much of a mess as yours. I am also a stranger to myself. How I feel inside is not how I act. I don't know who it is who acts, but it is not the person I am inside. I watch my behavior with horror, as if someone else were controlling me like a puppet. My heart is full of love, but I behave like a selfish, egotistical son of a bitch, like you. The fact is, most of the problems that plague human beings have no solution. One must simply live one's life while it's happening, and never allow the world or anyone in it make you ashamed of loving, or take away your ability to love. Despite the fact that it will probably kill you. When I finish this damned novel I'm going to give up fiction and write self-help books. But the Devil is a very cunning fellow. He keeps putting images in your head and whispering at you. Now he's whispering to me, kill her. Kill what you've created. Kill what you love. And I hear the train coming, and I want to save her. But somehow, the train comes, and she throws herself onto the tracks. I mourn for her. But I know in my heart that I am the one who killed her. In art, as in life, love is always fatal. So, what are you writing? No, don't tell me. It will just depress me.

Adam Kraar

Dramatic
Jed, sixteen

The play is set in a small town in Kansas. This scene takes place in the woods, by the mysterious remains of an old, abandoned car, an Impala. Jed is speaking to Manoah, a young woman of 15. He only met her recently, and is intrigued by her. But their previous encounter ended tensely, so now he's trying to impress her.

JED: This town was like a jewel. The factories—and the opera house—and the railroad—running full blast. Now, it's like a graveyard, with people smiling and nodding like zombies. You don't know what it used to be. The streets were like perfectly paved. There was a friggin' zoo! Now, it's just cages, and a smell. *(beat)* So this kid couldn't take it anymore. The silence of the zombies. So he hot-wires this car downtown, peels out, waking the dead. Turns out, it's the Mayor's Impala, which His Honor had souped up so he could speed off to other counties so he could drink on Sundays. Right away, the cops and the Highway Patrol give chase. He turns into the back alleys, trying to get out of town—if he can get to the Interstate, he's free. But they're cutting off every artery: Highway Patrol brings out the shotguns: every time he tries to get on Route One, they got a man with a 12 gauge. So finally this kid says, "Screw it." He charges out Peapod Alley, onto Main Street, and they open fire. He ducks, sidewinding, eighty, ninety miles an hour. By now, he's got two flats, black smoke pouring out the hood. No way he can get past these guys—it's suicide! But instead, he takes a mad right to Walnut. Heads straight out to the woods, drives off the road; tears up the ground, taking chunks outta trees, doesn't stop till his motor explodes – right here. . . . It's night now, and the whole woods light up like a nuclear fireball, brighter than day. When the cops get here, they figure he's burnt up. But they never found a body.

EVERYTHING'S FREE!
Sam Graber

Dramatic
Tyler, twenties

Desperate to have his credit card reactivated, and his girlfriend released from a credit card debt-induced catatonic state, Tyler begrudgingly reveals to a mysterious financial spirit guide his history with debt and homelessness.

TYLER: Alright. The short story is . . . my grandfather. Refugee from eastern Europe. Came to this country with nothing. The boats over were floating homeless shelters. All he had when he arrived was some torn clothes and a couple words of English. So with that he worked the streets, you know, you just survived. You survive long enough and you get ahead enough and you're not surviving anymore, you almost have a system of existence, you start to feel comfortable. Until the next boat arrives. And you see how you were when you landed, scared, lost, alone, the worst thing to feel in this world, alone. So my grandfather decided he was going to build places where the alone people like him could stay, and sleep, and learn. Twenty-four hours a day, where nobody felt alone. But how to do it. My grandfather said it came to him in a dream. To build a small building. That's all he said, a dream. But I knew what he meant. Back then you could just claim your life. People don't remember but we used to have those kind of small buildings. The long story is . . . Dad eventually decided what we had wasn't keeping up with the bigness of the world. You're either growing or dying, Dad said. So Dad took on debt and the debt took him until he couldn't take it anymore, all while pretending everything was okay. The day he left and never came back. The day the lights in the house stopped working. The day people took the house. The day I'm standing with Mom in a line to get . . . the card! For food. Mom said we'll be okay, Tyler, we'll figure out a way, we'll cut that card together. But soon Mom and I are standing in another line, this one for a place to sleep, and we didn't make it to the front. It was just one night. That's all it took, though, to feel on the streets how everyone's watching you. But no one's watching you. You're almost invisible to yourself at that point. Part of two different people but now belonging to neither. What happened was Mom found a warm spot, an alleyway with an air vent, but already there was a woman, crouched, cradling her infant baby. And we all just kind of looked at each other, without saying anything, like we were too terrified or embarrassed. It was the moment the baby . . . reached out its hand. This tiny hand. Like it needed every ounce of help the world could give to make its next breath. [Beat] My Aunt took us off the streets by the next morning. It was just one night. But every night since then is still me, standing in that alley, staring at that tiny hand, helpless and hopeless, like I can't break out of that moment. Even after Mom and I found a new system of existence, still that hand. Even after Mackenzie found me, made me feel visible again, who made me feel like I was wanted, with something to offer the world, still that hand. By the time we became who we are it was like who I am with you didn't need to mention that night. But I'm not here to sell advertising. I'm here for the people on the boat, my grandfather, my Mom, anyone who's ever had to put out that hand. But see . . . our bank says we're out of money. Our landlord's having us evicted. My bus driver wants to get paid. And my credit card doesn't work. But there's a lot of people out there who need help, who I'm helping. So I'm not going to give up. That's the long story: I'm not giving up.

For information on this author, click on the WRITERS tab at www.smithandkraus.com.

Dramatic
Palmer, not quite twenty-one.

Turner Street's bold paintings are the hottest thing to hit the scene – they've even captured the attention of the elusive Johanna, a journalist posing as a cater-waitress. Romance goes awry when his one-eyed, pill-popping, younger brother Palmer shows up at Turner's loft. After a night of Cain and Abel like fights and secrets being wretched open, Turner reveals to Palmer that their father didn't die fire-fighting but was a actually a drunk who committed suicide after years of abusing them and their mother, Palmer over-whelmed by grief and anger begins a tailspin, as he describes his decision to come to New York and the letter he thought Turner sent him, inviting him to his big gallery opening, the letter he just found out that it was actually forged by Johanna. Palmer wears a black eye patch over his left eye, which covers the scars from having lost his eye in a car accident as a child. Palmer is handsome and a charmer but has a boiling temper and propensity towards violence and addiction.

PALMER: No! See, you don't know what my life is like, what life really is in Eaton. In our home. What an invitation like that means. How it would feel. From your big brother. On fancy paper. Telling you to come to his big art show, telling you to come stay with him, telling you, you are welcome. And you think, no, it's no place for a fuck up like me. There's no place there for a screw up like me. You're not going to go. You barely got enough for a bus ticket as it is. Nothing's gonna change. *(Beat)* So you put it away. And you see him. Bill. In your room, going through your stuff. That you've worked so hard to get, your fix. And there he is. The man mom thinks will solve all the problems, the man who goes to church on Sundays, and fires up the grill, the man who sleeps in her bed. The man who says shit about you, and your brother, and Dad, and calls mom stupid. You watch as he pockets your stuff. Even swallows one, one of yours. The floor creaks. He sees you. He says, "What you gonna do about it, one-eye?" He grabs the letter, "New York City," he laughs. Spit flyin' from his mouth, says, "You're not going nowhere." And you're off. You are off. Grab the chair, dad's chair, the one with the spokes, the one Grandpa made, it's over your head and you are wailing on the fat fuck. You slam it and you slam it and you slam it, again and again until you feel it. You feel it. You feel the power, the completeness, the fire, and you feel it so much you don't feel the pain anymore. For a moment all that pain is gone. He's fallen, he's not moving, and you still keep going.

(Beat) A car rolls up outside. You hear the gravel under the tires. How long have I been? Is Mom home already? Did she bring me a slice of pie. Then you look down, at the bastards bloody kickball of a face. He's not moving. How long have I been? And you're out that door faster than a race horse. You are gone. And you feel like maybe . . . You've gone to far. You have nothing. *(long beat)* I have nothing.

Dramatic
Palmer, not quite 21.

*Turner Street's bold paintings are the hottest thing to
hit the scene – they've even captured the attention of
the elusive Johanna, a journalist posing as a cater-
waitress. Romance goes awry when his one-eyed,
pill-popping, younger brother Palmer shows up at
Turner's loft. After a night of Cain and Abel like fights
and secrets being wretched open, Turner reveals to
Palmer that their father didn't die fire-fighting but
was a actually a drunk who committed suicide after
years of abusing them and their mother, Palmer
overwhelmed by grief and anger begins a tailspin,
he's just described brutally murdering his step-father
with the spoke of a chair, and now holds Johanna at
knife point.Palmer wears a black eye patch over his
left eye, which covers the scars from having lost his
eye in a car accident as a child.*

PALMER: I believed you wanted to see me. I believed I mattered to you, to someone. I even brought my sketches.
Thought you'd even want to see them. In the bag! I can
draw too. Tell me what you think. Sure, they are no
pictures of my eye, I didn't need that to draw. You used
me. All of you. Used me. Everyone uses me, my eye,
my problems, my pills. All of you, use me. Everyone
needs to get their piece of me! Their fix. Bill used me,
used Mom, for my pills! Johanna, you used me for your
stupid story, to get to Turner, like I was a fucking carrot
hanging in front of the pony. Bring me all the way out
here. For him. For him. For him.

(to TURNER)

And you, you're worst of all. All these years, all the pain.

All the fights. All the things I've done, because of you. Because of what you did, and here you've been using me. Making something of me. Like I'm worthless.

(Palmer turns the knife to his own throat)

So here, I'm worthless. Like I'm some sort of thing you could kick around, beat to a pulp, because it makes you better. You painting me, my eye, makes you better. You use me! You use me, T, you use me! Turner! Look at you! Making money off of my eye. It's my eye. My eye. My eye!

Dramatic
Turner, early thirties

Turner Street's bold paintings are the hottest thing to hit the scene – they've even captured the attention of the elusive Johanna, a journalist posing as a cater-waitress. Romance goes awry when his one-eyed, pill-popping, younger brother Palmer shows up at Turner's loft. After a night of exposed secrets and Cain and Abel like fights between the brothers, Palmer attempts suicide by drug overdose, and Turner forces him to vomit. Palmer overhears Turner begin to tell Johanna why he caused the car accident that blinded his brother, and he interrupts by accusing Turner of crashing the car because he was jealous. Early in the play Palmer tells Johanna that their father died as a firefighter.

TURNER: Jealous? Of course I was. He'd sing you to sleep. And me? He'd tell me Nam stories at night. Yeah. He'd come to my bed and confess to me all the shit he did over there, and after when I couldn't sleep, he'd tell me The Sandman was coming, The Sandman was gonna cut out my eyes. It scared the shit out of me. He'd hurt [me]—Dad was a . . . . *(Pause.)* He ignored me. It was like I wasn't even there, unless he needed to confess his sins, or slap me around. Before I'd do a thing he'd whip out his belt and— Did he ever hit you? No? No. You were just this perfect son, could do no wrong, and better yet, you looked just like him. You shoulda' just waited, til' he stopped seeing you as his son and started seeing you as his rival, then you'da seen a different side of him. Dad was never going to leave Eaton. He was going to drink himself until everything other than

Eaton washed away. *(Beat)* Do you remember what you just did, Palmer? What you just did? One day no one is gonna be there to stop you. No one is gonna do that for you. One day you'll take it too far, the wrong combination, at the wrong place, at the wrong time. You need it. Right? Like Dad needed Schlitz and Jack? Like Dad needed blackouts and toilet hugs? Stomach pumps, and AA, and—That's you, Palmer! That's you! *(Beat)* Dad killed himself. Dad. Killed himself. He hung himself, Palmer. They didn't want to . . . Look, I was there. I was drawing in my room, and something just came over me, I wanted to show him how good I was. The door was open a crack, I even knocked. I went in, and there he was standing on the chair— I hadn't seen a bottle since he got sober last, but there was an empty bottle on the nightstand. The rope was attached to that sort of rusty beam, or that pipe thing. And he looked at me. He saw me. Looked me right in the eye. We connected in that stare, he knew I was there and I knew what was about to happen. Then he kicked the chair. I didn't know what to do. I didn't . . . I could've taken him down. Maybe done mouth to mouth, or I don't know. But I just thought about every time he hit me, every time he hit Mom, every time he got close around you, and I just watched him swing. I watched him until I was sure. And then I saw the note on the nightstand, next to the bottle. It said, of all things, "Sandman, bring me a dream." *(Beat)* In the car, you kept saying how he was a hero. Over and over and—The man I knew was a coward. A drunk. A . . . I couldn't deal with it. Letting him . . . Watching him . . . You started singing that song, and I don't know, but it all made sense. I hit the gas, headed for the tree, and just like dad . . . I was ready to sleep. *(Silence)* I didn't want you to find out this way. *(Beat)* Palmer? Palmer?

EYES SHUT. DOOR OPEN
Cassie M. Seinuk

Dramatic
Turner, early thirties

Turner Street's bold paintings are the hottest thing to hit the scene – they've even captured the attention of the elusive Johanna, who has an agenda of her own. This is the opening monologue from the play. Turner is holding a champagne flute at the gallery opening of his new collection. It seems like he is talking to the audience, but he is actually talking to a sultry and cool cater-waitress, Johanna, who is standing just out of the light. Turner is sexy, confident, and at the top of his game . . . or at least that's what he wants everyone, especially the art community, to think.

TURNER: You see me? You see! I'm everything to these people. That's right. You know, Van Goh, it's a fact, right, it's a fact that he didn't break-through, he didn't have his break-though, his success, until he . . . you know. But see I've reached that place where they look at me, and I'm still all intact. I can actually see it. Be a part of it. If I want to, I mean. They are looking, aren't they? And they want me. They want to have my art. They want to be my art. But I'm not talking to them. No. I'm not looking at them. I'm looking at you. See that's my "now." My current rung in the ladder. Best part is, they have no idea what they are looking at. But they'll talk about it, until they're tongues dry out. And I'll watch them, I'll take a peak, because it's fun. They'll never know the truth, the real meaning, the pulse behind the art itself, and that's what's fun, right? They'll see something, but not the real thing. And they throw down their check books. That's when you know. And when you know you're hot, they want you.

Dramatic

Abel, early thirties, Mexican American

Abel is a janitor at a film studio. He has become friends with Lucia, a writer. Abel was married, but not anymore.

ABEL: I didn't know she would turn out to be a *liona*. She was on her best behavior right up until we moved into our own place in Boyle Heights. Then she turned into a real . . . But it was okay for us and for like around six months everything was good. Pretty nice actually. And then, I don't know what happened but she started — truth be told is I think she was sniffing, but I still can't prove that. She had this aunt that came to live with us and she would always start drama with us. And the thing is, it was like affecting the baby. She'd leave with her aunt God-knows-where and I'd come home and the baby would be all alone, crying in the crib. But if I would say anything, the both of them would pounce on me. *Para no hacertela larga* we split up and then it got, just, it got bad. *La Tia*, she came to my job, not here, I used to be a fireman, actually, so she came to the firehouse, *y armo un desmadre* saying that "this and that," that now that she had her citizenship she was going to take the baby back to El Salvador and not tell me where. And like other shit. They were also taking money from my account and wouldn't tell me for what. Just shady shit. I don't know what the two of them were into, who even knows if that lady was even her aunt, you know? I think about that now. Was she even her *tia*? Anyway, one day *la tia* comes to my work and says that they're leaving that day. So I run over there and all her cousins — well, that's who she says they are, but I never met no cousins of her's before—they're like six of them in the front yard. And something didn't look right. The whole thing—God, I've played it back in my mind, over and over. Drove me nuts while I was locked up. Something just wasn't right that day. Anyway, I go in and she's like half dressed and all wyled out. Sweaty and hyper. The baby crying on the floor there with like two big Salvatrucha looking dudes. They just looked like it to me. Could have been her cousins but I don't know. I didn't want to find out. I just wanted my baby. So I start telling Silvia—that was my ex's name—I tell her that she can't take my baby. That I won't let her take her. And let me tell you, hell really hath no fury. This bitch, she's about this big but she can get crazy. Throwing shit, spitting out things you wouldn't even write on a bathroom wall. The MS dudes give us some space I guess because they go outside. And I grab Melita and try to get her diaper bag to just take her away while Silvia calms down. But as soon as I do that, the fucking Tia comes out of no where and starts beating me with the fucking curling iron and then Silvia just goes nuts and grabs a knife. And she starts waving that thing around. So I'm trying to make my way out the door, but I got the aunt beating me and then Silvia slashing at me. Cutting deep too. And then she stabs me. Like for real. And I say to her, "I got the baby in my arms you fucking maniac! What the fuck is wrong with you?!" No consideration for the baby in my arms. What if she stabbed her? But that bitch won't listen cuz she's like an animal. And when she's about to lunge at me again I just punch her right on the nose. I mean, I just floored her. Blood squirting everywhere. The *tia* comes at me and I round house that fucking bitch too. Nobody's caring about Melita, these fucking bitches. My poor baby in my arms, hysterical. Imagine having to see that? That baby is my whole world. I don't give a fuck if it's her mother, I won't let nobody hurt her.

Dramatic
Owen, thirty to thirty-five

Owen, is a guidance counselor. He is a good-natured man with the air of an ex-jock, but not an unintelligent one. He is talking to Theresa, a single mother in her early 30's, and decides to make one last attempt to learn why she ended their relationship several months before. (He's also recently been told by an angel to strive to be a good man.)

OWEN: You know what, I don't need this anymore.

(He starts for the front door, then stops. He comes back, defiantly.)

This is what you always do, you piss me off so I never get anywhere. Well, I'm a good man, okay!? I mean, a good man wouldn't let himself get all deflected, a good man would get somewhere and I'm gonna be a good man tonight. So you tell me why you broke up with me cuz I need to know. (Pause; no response) When Simon was away on that school band trip, you jumped my bones as soon as we came in the door from Olive Garden, and it was, like, so intense and so good, I couldn't even sleep after. *(Pause)* So I lay there, watching you sleep, watching your chest go up and down like these gentle waves were rolling under you. I never knew you could look so peaceful. And that's when I knew, Therese, that's when I knew for sure, I was completely falling in love, and then suddenly, you woke up, and you flipped out, and told me I had to go, and I had no idea what had had happened. *(Pause)* And don't pretend you were worried that Simon wasn't going to find us in bed. Simon wasn't even gonna be home for, like, 12 hours! At some point, doesn't he need to get used to you having a guy over?

(Pause) So, I'm gonna ask you one more time: why did you break up with me?

Seriocomic
Francis Darling, mid-thirties

*Francis, a neurosurgeon, is speaking to his wife
Wendy in the final hours of his life.*

FRANCIS: I think the world is coming apart, Wendy. I think
it's coming undone - there's atrophy, a hemorrhaging
—I can feel it. I know we've always said that, each
generation repeating those words like it's a brand new
totally original thought—like for some reason we're
closer to the coming-apart-of-life than the generation
last, the same way *they* talked about their own perceived
unprecedented nearing of doom, with drills and sirens
and giant clocks. But I swear to you, Wendy, I can *feel*
it coming, and believe me, that alone doesn't scare me
so much as something else entirely. Wendy, in this fine
century made of screaming plastic, it seems to me that
we are all ready and able and willing to finish ourselves
off. It's like we're not interested in holding it together. I
know, it doesn't make much sense - it doesn't make any
sense to me either, but it seems that's the case. There
are signs, Wendy - I can see it everywhere—it's in the
blinking of the traffic lights. Wendy, yesterday, when
we were watching television, we saw Britney's new
music video that has her straddling a giant tank. I don't
even know for what reason or purpose, I don't know
if there's a message there, but anyway, no one said a
word about it, not even a peep. No one thought to ask,
"what's going on there, huh?" I mean, did you see the
bodybuilding championships and the football games
and the ultimate fighting champions and all the wars,
fictional and real, on TV? Did you see how none of us

said anything about all that, you and me and the kids? We could have *said* something about it. Like, "why do I enjoy ultimate fighting champions this much?" or "why is she on that tank, I mean, I like it, but why?" but there was nothing. Wendy, I fear there is no longer a people. I fear we just want to forget for one moment that we are people—at least, that we were people once, once upon a time, in a faraway land. Now every moment seems to be a wailing attempt to have a moment of silence. And really, in this heavy silence, in this desperate situation held together with industrial glue, how could they expect us to be interested in anything but the present fifty second video of a cute cat? Wendy, the first three words out of our children's mouths were "mommy" and "genocide" and "XBOX 360."What do you think that means, Wendy? What do you think that means?

For information on this author, click on the WRITERS tab at www.smithandkraus.com.

Comic
Djuna, twenties-thirties

Djuna and Mel are the last two people on earth. The question is, will they have sex and begin to re-populate the planet? Mel is reluctant – she's more concerned with survival. She has caught Djuna masturbating (yuck). Here's his response.

DJUNA: Obviously I masturbate. It's been 19 months, we're alive, we're healthy, we're not gonna. But the point is. Without being too accusatory or pressure-y. Because we can table this discussion for now, we really can. But the point is, I know your sex drive isn't gone. Mine's not gone. And I know you don't want to have sex with me. I don't particularly want to have sex with you either. It's really hard to want to have sex with somebody who has spent the better part of the last year and a half alternately crying and screaming at you. NOT THAT I BLAME YOU FOR THAT. I mean we aren't in a sexy situation. When I masturbate I don't close my eyes and think of you. I close my eyes and think of a house, and a bed, and like. A college girl with bouncy tits and she's worried about finals and I'm her tutor and she pays me in blow jobs. I don't want to have sex with you, Mel! But here's what I do want, I do want to have sex. I *want* to have sex. And I want to eat food. And I want to watch a movie. And I want to feel flannel sheets on my skin and play a game on my phone and talk to my mom again. And nooooone of these things are gonna happen. None of them. And, you know, we could die of radiation in a month, we could be dying right now—OR! Or. We could be just fucking fine. And have another, I dunno, thirty years here. And at some point it's like. I don't know, at what point do you decide that you're done just surviving and you're gonna. Give yourself something. Of course it's not going to be good! It's going to be just as awkward and weird as you think it will be. And then maybe we don't do it again for months. Years. Decades, who knows.

Dramatic
Hale, forties

Tanner Hale is a head football coach who finds his major college program threatened by a potential sex scandal. Hale is speaking to Toby, a graduate assistant who reported having seen one of the team's coaches in a sexual situation with a teenage boy.

HALE: Ever think about our fight song? Last line, for example. "For the loyal, the brave and true". Three concepts in that line, and the first one is loyalty. Know what that says? You can't be brave unless you're loyal first. Hell, you wouldn't know who to be brave for. You can't be true unless you're both loyal and brave. Mitch Carlson is not loyal. He's loyal to his dick, not to this program. You have a dick; I have a dick. I suppose we like to think we're loyal to our dicks. But not above team. Not above the program. Mitch should have cut his dick off before he pledged allegiance to it above this program. Now I have to cut it off for him. One of my oldest friends. Shit. This is why I get paid millions of dollars. This, right here. If you're gonna build an empire, you gotta act like an emperor. Gotta spill blood. Remember this Toby, your whole career. Program. Loyalty. *Then* your dick. Okay. I'll meet you at your house in half an hour. I'll pick up Mitch on the way. Tell your wife we're going out to talk over hiring you full-time. Don't tell her anything else. She's just a wife. She will not understand. So easy to knock a program like ours—to forget all the good. Boys who'd never be able to think of college, you know? We get 'em a degree. Kids from poor families, bad families—no families. They've got one talent in the world.

We make sure it buys 'em something. That's what we're about. Loyalty, Toby. It's the air we breathe.

Dramatic
Jackson, late twenties-early thirties

Jackson and Emma are hours away from signing divorce papers. Here, Jackson is having dinner with Emma, as well as Emma's sister, Sophia. Sophia has asked, one too many times, if there's any way that Emma and Jackson can avoid a divorce.

JACKSON: You know why people ask the same question over and over? Either they don't like the answer, or they don't want to believe the answer. So listen up, kiddoes, here's the real and true answer. Emma and I will not reconcile. And here is why. Pay attention Sophia, this is the good stuff. Say we live in a world where divorce doesn't exist. Poof. That's where we are now. Emma and I must stay together, no matter what. We are forced to be a married couple forever and ever. Emma and I stay together, growing more and more distant every day. I get a dog, she gets more cats. Each of us builds a world where the other exists only on the edges. At the exclusion of any real affection, any real love, we haunt our home, along with the ghosts of the people we used to be. Our home is divided. I take the study, she gets the den. That's where we go when we don't want to be reminded of the presence of the other. The living room, the room where we used to stay up late and watch marathons of really bad TV, Emma's an expert at finding the worst stuff, the living room is now the DMZ—a place to pass through . . . without really looking at the couch where I used to rub her feet . . . the chair where she'd read me the crossword puzzle clues . . . That is where our ghosts live. Don't look at them directly or they will consume you. We'd share a haunted house, Emma and I to the exclusion of any future possible happiness. Is your question answered now, Sophia?

For information on this author, click on the WRITERS tab at www.smithandkraus.com.

Seriocomic
Gene, thirty-five

*1923. Playwright Eugene O'Neill runs into his
friends, critic Edmund Wilson, and poet Edna St. Vincent Millay, on MacDougal Street in Greenwich Village one evening, having had too much to drink and
proclaiming angrily to everybody within earshot
that he is not the Count Of Monte Cristo, the role
his actor father played for years, in a very mediocre
play, to make money. O'Neill says very little when
sober, but when drunk he is quite a different fellow.
He is angry at critics and the commercial theatre
establishment, but in a larger sense he's angry at
an American culture which worships stupidity and
destroys what is good in its best artists. He is increasingly passionate here, and believes deeply what he
builds to at the end. He is trying to save their lives
and souls as artists.*

GENE: The sons of bitches praise you for the worst in you and
attack you for the best. Let's all get together and help you
fix up your play, Mr O'Neill. Of course, I myself couldn't
write my way out of a paper bag if my life depended on
it, but I know better than you what your play should be
because John Barrymore once screwed my sister in the
prop room. Just do the second act backwards and put
in some tap dancing and a sword fight. And make sure
every damned character tells us exactly why he's doing
everything so my feeble minded Aunt Sadie won't have
any trouble knowing what she's supposed to think. I
didn't become a playwright so I could sit in a hotel room
in New Haven at four in the morning doing rewrites with
a sub-literate producer with enough hair to fabricate a

Pekinese growing out his nose and a director with the intelligence of a sea cucumber. Get your brain sucked out by a ground sloth? No problem. Come and write theatre criticism for the *New York Times*. The beauty of it is, you don't even need to go to the fucking plays. You can stay home all night fornicating with your Saint Bernard and stuffing walnuts up your ass. Praise and blame is a game for cretins, and fame is a rotting, disease-ridden whore. It will devour you. They're all cannibals out there. If they can't stop you writing altogether, they try to make you one of them, bully you into puking out the sort of crap they would write if they had the balls to write what you write. And if they can't get you to write crap, the fuckers try to kill you. And if you wake up some morning and look in the mirror and see one of them looking back at you, you might just as well blow your damned brains out then and there, because all you've got is your work. Don't listen to these cockroaches. Never make excuses. Never try to justify. Never explain. Never give in to them. Just do your work. Do exactly what feels right to you, no matter what anybody says, and fuck everything else. The only salvation is your work. Forget that for one second, and your soul is dead forever.

THE GRASS IS GREENEST AT THE HOUSTON ASTRODOME

Michael Ross Albert

Dramatic
Pablo, early twenties

The unpaid intern of a floundering independent art gallery confronts Caroline, a jealous painter who has destroyed his artwork in a fit of rage, and who has recently discovered that her fiancée has had an affair with another man.

PABLO: I'm sick and tired of you screaming at everyone, Caroline. Regardless of what your, you know, justification, given the circumstances, might be. I couldn't really hear what you were saying back there, but I figure it's probably true that Marshall and John did, in fact, like, hook up even if I couldn't necessarily . . . I mean, the volume of your voice carries even if the acoustics are, whatever, even if I couldn't hear every word you were . . . I mean . . . Damn it, I had everything I wanted to say planned out before I came over here and now it's not coming out right. Why are you always so dismissive of me? I know I'm not cool like other sculptors. I'm not suave. I'm not earthy and manly and don't, like, casually wear clothes that show off my big muscles, don't grow my hair down to my shoulders. But I'm still an artist, and I still have a right to talk, and I still think you need to know that even if you have just cause in this one particular instance, you need to learn that if you treat people like shit, of course no one's going to want to make a long-term romantic commitment to you. I know you all think of me as just the intern because I didn't graduate in the same year as you and because I'm . . . I dunno, I had a whole big speech sort of welling up back there and now that I'm out here I don't really think I'm making it sound convincing, but I want you to know that I think it's time someone took a stand and tried to make you nicer. Just be *nicer* to people. Why do you have to be mean? Because you're an artist?

The Grass Is Greenest At The Houston Astrodome

Michael Ross Albert

Dramatic
John, late twenties/early thirties

A scientist engaged to a female artist confesses the details of a secret romantic encounter with Marshall, her friend and colleague.

JOHN: Klimt. I like that guy. Although he was mostly active before the . . . Anyway. I talked about all the things I knew about that period, all those new things I started trying to teach myself about art since I came back from Chicago. And it wasn't until we were leaving the gallery, getting our coats at coat check, that Marshall told me he was an artist himself. I wasn't going to, to text him again or see him again because I felt, when we were together, that I'd much rather be with you, but there was something . . . I wanted to know more about him, and his work, and if it would . . . if *that* was what I was drawn to. Not him as a man, but him as an artist. So we went for a drink, and I kept asking Marshall about his work, and he's really not lying when he says he doesn't like talking about it, it took a fair bit of coercing. But finally around our third beer, he told me about this piece he was working on.

(to MARSHALL)

Do you mind if I talk about it? See, Marshall's dad was from Texas. He was a minor league baseball player. Except an injury kept him, kept him from playing professionally. He told me this thing his dad used to say. This non sequitur. See, we were talking about being disenchanted with our jobs (lately I've been feeling a bit dissatisfied at work, maybe it's the winter, this cold) and I was saying, "I wish I had the ability to create something like you do." And he said he wished he had something like my job.

Something stable, something that (even though it hasn't felt this way to me in a while) something that makes a difference in our city. Something . . . satisfying. A reason to get out of bed in the morning and feel useful. It might seem perfect on the outside, but . . . But I haven't felt that way in a while. And I said to Marshall, "I guess the grass is always greener on the other side of the fence." And Marshall said, he told me this thing his dad used to say, this old saying of his . . . And that was the title of Marshall's new piece. "The Grass is Greenest at the Houston Astrodome." I don't know if I can . . . It's like . . . No matter how, how badly you think you want something . . . I'm not really putting this well. The grass is greenest at the . . . It's like. Our dream of perfection is a dream of something that doesn't exist. It's fake. It's not real. It's made to fool us into thinking that there is actually something more . . . desirable than what we've got right now. And now this place (I looked it up in the news after you and I talked about it) this seemingly perfect place —- the greenest grass is all gone. Like it never existed in the first place.

Dramatic
Drew, forty-eight

Drew is a software engineer who developed the early software for the Predator Drone Program. His son, Nathan, joins the Army and is killed by a friendly-fire U.S. drone. Drew attempts to explain to Nathan his complicity in Nathan's death

DREW: I wrote that source code when I was a kid. Your age. It was the control loop, the firmware, the early prototype for the chips that evolved into part of the Predator Drone. The unmanned aerial vehicles we dreamed would separate the human from the equation. Save lives. So many lives. We wrote it because of Vietnam. Hitler. The Civil War. We had no idea what the early artificial intelligence program would become. That was before we could really imagine all it could do. When it felt like some kind of grown-up videogame that we were being paid to write. Fun. I wrote it then. I wrote it sloppily because I was trying to get out of work early that day. It's the only thing that makes any sense. I was trying to get out of work early. To meet a girl. Her name was Cheryl. Cheryl Alston. Who later became your mother. And later, Shanti. Who kept transforming herself. While we stayed behind and remained the same old people. The ones she promised her life to. You and me. I was going to meet her. And I remember that day. Specifically. Because I had a question about it. My code. I had a question about one part. And I thought. I'll do it later. I'll get to it on Monday. It was a Friday and there was a weekend. And Shanti, I mean, Cheryl. I had put her off. And she was getting fed up with me. She was claiming my job was more important than she was. She was claiming all these things about me. And we had a date to a museum. Where everything was white. The edifice. The building. The walls. The marble. The art. Snow balancing itself on the trees and the grass outside. A wonderful world of white. In Washington DC. And the only color in it was your mother. She was the only color. There. I knew I had to go. I knew I had to catch that train. Because if I missed it. If I missed this. I might be condemned to a dull life. And, son, I never wanted a dull life. Not for anyone. Not for her. Not for you. So, I hit Save and I told myself I'd be back on Monday. And Monday came and a new task came in and I was diverted there. At least, I would like to think I was diverted. I'd like to believe that. Someone else stole my attention. I'd like it to be some other person's fault. Than my own. It was a snowy white day in Washington DC. And I fell in love with your mother. That day. And that killed you. My son.

Dramatic
Nathan, twenty-four.

Nathan, a soldier, was killed by a friendly-fire preda-tor drone. His father, Drew, was the Project Lead in developing drone warfare. After he dies, Nathan sees his father one more time.

NATHAN: You don't get to do that. You don't get to quit like that. You don't get to die. You get to live. So, you better fucking take it, Dad. You better fucking take your opportunity. You'd better seize the day you lived and I didn't. You'd better go back to the Mall and take her hand. You'd better look Shanti-mother in the face and tell her how you really feel. You'd better lift her up into the air. And toss her really high. And be there. To fuck-ing catch her. Like you promised. In the first place. But you'd better catch her. This time. You'd better *change* for her. Because people can change. Regret can make them into somebody else. And if you ever do anything with your life. It better be this. To become a better man. Because of me.

(Takes a beat, changes, as if in command)

That's an order. Live like you've got balls, Dad. Live like you fucking mean it. Live like it would kill you to do anything else. Live for me.

Dramatic
Salvy, forties

Salvy is a hitman for the mob., tough and irascible,
but with a soft spot for his family. His cousin, Casmir,
is a screenwriter who is being ripped off by a ruth-
less film producer. Salvy visits his anguished cousin
to give him a good pep talk.

SALVY: Don't you know how to stand up to this asshole? You
gotta look this shit in the face. You gotta pull out all the
stops on this cocksucker, if it means your last breath.
Then and only then can you sit there and tell me you
really tried. Like this badass I worked for. This moth-
erfucka made the devil run the otha way. I took 'is shit,
everybody took 'is shit. He'd smack people around,
spit in their faces. Rumor has it he spit on little Nicky
Scarfo's shoes. He became Scarfo's right hand, within
a year he's *caporegime.* Ya know why? Dis fucka had
balls o' concrete. Like Michelangelo's David, know what
I mean? Cocksucka whacks my best friend. Wit 'is chick
no less. Found 'em naked in 'is bed, smiles across their
faces. So I walk into the back of 'is joint, unannounced.
Fucker's sprinklin' red pepper on 'is veal, and I tol'
'im, right in front of 'is goons, I tol' 'at mothafucka
good. I said, "You mothafucker-- I'm gonna rip out your
fuckin' soul and sell it to the devil with a discount. You
cocksuckin', mothafuckin', pig fuckin' scum-- I eat ya
motha's pussy an' I spit it in you fatha's face! Who the
fuck you think you are to kill my friend?!" He looked
at me. One o' those looks, he didn't know what hit 'im.
Then his eyes, those black shark's eyes, staring right
into me. I's waitin' for a wire 'round my neck but I knew
he'd never do nutin' in his own joint. Dis mothabanger

was waitin' for me to crack. The silence-- the silence felt like forever. Ya could hear a pin drop. And I didn't even blink. Then his cheeks-- his cheeks opened up and this grin-- this wide grin spread across 'is face. It was then I knew! That I was in. I went to that which I was most afraid of and tore into it. Now can you say as much for yourself? Did you try that hard? Dis producer, this worthless piece o'shit who's fuckin' wit ya. You gotta do the same. I'm sure he ain't half the man I had to do it to. No, these guys you're talkin' about they fight wit' pencils and phones. Let me tell you somethin', real men don't fight wit' pencils and phones. They fight wi.t these! They use these things, these long things, to rip and tear. This part here to smack and humiliate. Squeeze 'em all together, ya knock skulls in!

(Slams his fist down on the table.)

And, let me tell ya, they never stop until they see blood!

For information on this author, click on the WRITERS tab at www.smithandkraus.com.

Dramatic
Hendricks, thirty-forty

*Lenny Hendricks is a bar-fly and a WWII veteran.
He's been back from the war for a few years. He
wasn't much of a man before he left, and he's even
less now that he's back. His actions during the war
come back to haunt him when a private investigator,
to whom he is speaking here, starts to look into what
happened during his last fire-fight.*

HENDRICKS: There's a tinny taste you get in your mouth
during a gun fight. Before it even starts. Adrenaline. I
guess a lot of people know that. Different from the taste
of blood in your mouth. That's a different kind of metal.
I don't know. Copper? I don't know. But in a foxhole—
they don't tell you this—maybe you're supposed to just
know—what you smell is dirt. And salt. And wet. And
if there's that metal taste, it's nothing, just an aftertaste
when all is said and done. If you can get past the taste
of the dirt. I still taste it. Not a taste you could forget,
really. And the body's a stubborn bastard. Doesn't seem
to want to taste anything else. It's like—what's that Bible
story? Where the fruits taste like ashes in their mouths?
I can't remember what God was punishing them for ... I
don't tell this story very often. In fact, I can't remember
the last time I told it. *(Beat)* I never killed a man. I was
over there for three years and I don't think my hands
ever stopped shaking long enough to fire a shot. Never
killed anyone. Except one guy. We were a few miles
from Verrieres Ridge. It was—this sounds stupid when
I say it out loud but—it was the loudest night of my life.
Everything after it for months was like my head was
under water. I couldn't—We shouldn't've even been

there. Some Canadian divisions were supposed to take the Ridge and we were there in support and suddenly you couldn't see the Canadian line, you couldn't see anything, and the lieutenant is yelling to advance and it's me and Bobby in the foxhole and the rest of the line is already paired up and headed into the smoke. I ran. And when I got to the tree line I looked back and there wasn't any foxhole and I guess there wasn't any Bobby anymore. And I kept running til I hit this barstool.

For information on this author, click on the WRITERS tab at www.smithandkraus.com.

Comic
Ethan, thirties

Ethan is talking to Daphne, trying to woo her, to impress her with his ability to understand himself and his past and how it has made him the man he is today. He is earnest, passionate and self-assured. This is a flirtatious yet confessional moment for him.

ETHAN: If you really want to know, fine, I'll tell you, it's a simple story, amusing, okay, here we go: I wanted to be a doctor, my mother wanted me to be a waiter. I want to learn about the heart, she wants me to serve artichoke hearts with a garlic aioli dipping sauce. I eventually caved and found the best restaurant in town: I walked in and am like, "I want to be a waiter. *Here.*" And he's like, "You have no experience." And I looked him in the eye and am like, "Okay man, I'll be a busser." And he's like "No." And I'm like "I will be a dishwasher." And he's like "No." And I'm like "okay—I'll be a FREE dishwasher." And he's like… "No." I don't tell that to many people … It never would have happened without your encouragement, Daphne. Your persistence. Your enthusiasm. Your cool hair. I was at a convention. Before the book, in real life, after I left Zenn-La. There was a presentation by: A Man. He spoke for hours and hours on the subject of life, of love, of How To Get Into Buildings. There was fire, images, music. There was something strangely intriguing about him. There actually was a fire, so I never heard the end of his speech but I *trusted* him. There was a sadness behind his eyes and a fierceness to his cadence, he inspired and endeared. He spoke about the uniform of a Pizza Delivery Guy. About its potential. He spoke, and I listened.

Comic
Roger, twenties

This is Roger's Big Moment. He is finally presenting his presentation at Comic Con this year – it's his guide to survival for the modern man or woman. He believes deeply in his well developed philosophies and has been waiting for this moment, the platform where he will share his ideas with the world...

ROGER: Good afternoon Ladies and Gentlemen, Super Heroes and Lords of the Underworld...What people, today, in our society, on Earth, don't realize is, that most buildings are just that: *Buildings.* They are buildings with *people* in them. You, or One, may for instance, just walk in the door. Just go into a building and say: "Hey is the superintendent around?" And they're like, "What?" And you say, more forcefully, "Hey—is the super here." And sometimes they say, "No, come back after lunch." And you should just say "cool" or something and just hang out for a bit, outside or at Starbucks and then, go back after lunch and start it all again. *Persistence.* You may think you know what you want to "study" or "be" but I'm telling you right now, don't go running around like a child saying "I'm going to be a Doctor when I grown up." Because you'll be lucky if you're a Waiter. *Lucky. So, Stop speculating everyone*! You know? Right now you're all just *speculating. Speculating.* The great thing that I was never told and that I wish I knew at a much younger age is this: The world is just a bunch of people dude. You have to be ready to BE one of them. And you can be annoying or persistent—that's totally fine! One way modern men, and women, meet people is to dress as a common Pizza Delivery Guy, or Gal, and enter a building. Tips to ensure entrance include: Make sure you carry the pizza box as if there is a pizza inside. People apparently will let someone with a Pizza in ANYWHERE. "I'm here to see Mr. Carmichael on the 21st floor." "Go right up." "Nancy from accounting ordered a deep dish Hawaiian, which floor is she on again?" "11. Lucky Nancy!" Whether there's a pizza actually IN the box or not, that's up to you. Because you are just a dude trying to figure out a way into a building. Into a club. It's one big club, and with persistence, if you stop speculating, and if you show up ready to deliver a pizza, you'll have a fair chance of getting in. So, be sure you show up with a pizza box and get ready for a waterfall effect or snowball effect of life's big elements to start happening to you. They'll be like:

Grab a chair!

There's your desk!

Here's your cool new cards!

That's your phone!

Meet your wife!

There's your kids!

Board meeting at noon!

Last one to the diner has to buy! *Now look at you.* You're in the building, in the club, hell you're on your way to being President of the club. I for one, couldn't be more proud because it's an awful world out there, but look at you, you just made it. You made it.

Dramatic
Dan, twenties

Dan is in a relationship with a woman he really cares about, and he doesn't want her to feel as badly as she does. He's speaking to the audience.

DAN: My girlfriend watches these procedural TV shows. She watches like a dozen of them at a time, in a marathon. She won't talk to me either, while she watches. If I try to talk she glares at me, or turns up the volume, or just says: Stop! I don't mean to watch but I like to sit next to her while she's quiet like that, I like to watch her while she watches. On all of these shows there's like a really crazy bad person who likes to hurt people and like the only way this person can get any joy is to hurt people, children mostly, and women. But it's not like they even get any joy, they just have this compulsion to be mean to people. It's like they want to see this pain on a child's face so maybe they don't feel so alone in their pain or whatever. So what happens is you feel anxiety about the child, while simultaneously feeling sympathy with the bad guy, and these two things sit in your heart and conflict. You don't Want anything to happen to the kid, but you Understand this guy. And looking back into the bad guy's life you feel bad for him in his victim hood childhood, while simultaneously understanding the bad guy who did this to him. When you think about it like that it feels very, it feels like there's nothing you can do, that the cycle is endless, that we just have to go around understanding and feeling bad for all these fucked up people forever. It feels like we just have to sympathize with everyone cause everyone has their reasons. Writers write that shit. They think we want to watch it—and we do watch it. But here's the deal: we watch it because that conflict in our chests is addictive, feeling things in a powerful way is addicting, and we want to feel things is a powerful way. But we don't really want to watch kids being hurt anymore, and we don't want to hear any more psychological excuses as to why a man would hurt a child. Just Stop. Let us fill our chests with something else.

Dramatic
Johnny, mid to late forties

Johnny is a ghost who haunts his sister Audrey.
Johnny died just a few days ago in the farm house in
North Dakota where he, a talented artist, got stuck on
the family farm. In this scene, he speaks to his sister,
whose husband just walked out the door. Audrey is
grieving Johnny's death, the end of her marriage,
and the fact that she fled the farm for the city but
never developed herself as an artist.

JOHNNY: You want to go after him? What'll that prove?
Won't prove love. If what you're feeling is love – and it
probably is—it'll always be there, like a penny in your
back pocket. Fine, have it your way, go after him. Keys
are in the ignition, but that ol' pick-up won't go over
forty-five without a battle. We're not followers. I was
too stubborn to follow a woman who was so audacious
as to take my child. We're cut from the same cloth,
sister. No wonder we're screwed. Products of a mixed
marriage: Norwegian and Swede, held together with
stoicism and guilt when you're having fun. You want to
ask: "How'd you do it, Johnny? How'd you stay here
all these years?" I painted, just to bring some color into
this frozen landscape. This is as good a place as any for
grieving. Something about watching a growing season
that gives you hope. A farm is kind of like a piece of art.
It's not obvious. You look out the window and think,
when did those stalks of wheat get that tall? You're painting and you can't see what you have until you step away.
No crop is like the one before it. Start a new painting, no
idea if it's going to turn out. In ten minutes a hail storm
can destroy a crop that's been growing for three months.
In two minutes, after painting for two weeks, I could pick

up the canvas, open the window in that studio, throw it outside, run down the stairs, go out and grab a fistful of mud and throw it on the picture. Don't think I haven't done that. Selling the farm, it's one of the hardest decisions a person . . . someone's gotta do it sometime. Do it when the time is right, Audrey, but not before. When you know in your heart it's time, then light the lamps and torch the place. . . . Sleep, sister, for tomorrow's a big day. Tomorrow you'll take stock of your new ... situation. I think it's already tomorrow, isn't it?

Dramatic
Kyle, early twenties, any ethnicity

Kyle, a young soldier, sits crouched in hiding in a camp that is under mortar attack. Scared and alone, he sends a letter home to his brother.

KYLE: Listen, I don't know what happened with the Skype, but I gotta get this to you man, they gon' cut us off in a minute. Told us to travel light but this some heavy-ass shit, these bitches ain't playin. *(Pause)* Fraid I'm 'on blow up, fuck up, get shot, get my dick blowed off. How in the entire fuck did you deal with this, brother? I can't even believe you want *back . . .* second tour*?* Renata's gon leave-yo-ass, or kill you these motherfuckers don't.

   (Beat)

Listen, Mitch, man . . . I'm 'on keep it real here for a minute. You 'member that time I shit myself in third grade—I can't even believe I'm—fuck it, lemme say it. You 'member you drove to school and got me home and cleaned me up and shit 'fore pop got home? Cried like a motherfucker, I ain't never been so scared. But 'member you tol' me it ain't matter? You said it was ok to be scared, sound just like pop, you said a *man who knows fear, knows himself.*

   (Beat)

I ain't ever forget that, brother. Is it snowing up in Brooklyn . . . down in Brooklyn . . . whereverthefuck Brooklyn . . .

   (Falling apart)

I ain't ever gon see my baby, he ain't even know my face.

(Beat)

Just do me a solid, man, if I don't make it back. Check on Boo and take my truck, my Jordans, hell, take it all, man, take it all . . .

(He closes his eyes and rocks softly.)

I love you. I love you, man.

Dramatic
Jimmy, twenty-four

Jimmy challenges his agent Jane's warning.

JIMMY: I know I defied the contracts. I needed to perfect the script . . . to be true to my talent, to follow a higher standard than those producers were using. Yes, I rewrote my lines and hit the director. It was war. I knew the part better than he did. And he wasn't used to an actor being smart. *(Pause)* I can't be part of a group of dopes. Let them take the guts out of me. What's an actor without guts? You should come to my dressing room and take your turn on the gallows. Sleep sitting up, six pillows behind your back, a gun in your pocket. Always ready for their bushwhack. I don't care about their profits or paperwork. I won't be remembered as a minor talent. I thought I'd found myself in you, Jane, so when you didn't side with me . . . when you arrived on the set like the wandering Picasso, .I attacked you! Look, Jane, I'm obsessed. I broke 3 fingers hitting that desk in *Rebel*--I was exhausted. I had to do movies back to back. And race in between . . . I needed to "not think" to bust open my memories- I should have stopped making movies when I got depressed. Helped other actors make movies so they could get depressed. Do you know what it's like to finish a movie! It's like being on a bus that crashes into a stone wall. And yes, I'm haunted by nightmares—and day mares . . . when I do movies . . . because . . . because . . . When I do movies it seems to me that I'm carrying a very fragile treasure. A fish that's in the water has no choice than to be what he is. Genius would have it that he swim in sand. We are fish and we drown.

Dramatic
Adam, twenties

Adam talks to himself and the audience before attending a wedding rehearsal dinner with his high school crush.

ADAM: I miss how handsome I used to be. I miss how effortless everything seemed and was. I miss playing. And grabbing a rebound on the basketball court. The feeling of leather on my palms And the sound of my name echoing in a gymnasium I miss enthusiasm. And desire. The feeling of desire For the moment. For the future For every girl I meet .I miss gliding through the hallways unaware of my own beauty as my limbs- they moved me effortlessly from classroom to classroom to practice to my car and I would drive it-the windows down while the air tussled my hair. And I would be so handsome. I mean, I'm not a bad looking guy now. Sure. But back then. Shit. Was I handsome. And now I miss it like I miss drinking alcohol without regret and going fast without consequence. And dancing hard unaware that there might not be a tomorrow. I miss my best friend who died of a heroin overdose. These days I'm thinking that I should have worked harder. Tried harder. Been more joyful. Traveled more. Took better care of my hair I hope it doesn't thin like my father's gee I hope my belly doesn't swell. Do I diet? Do men diet? And my feet do they smell and my teeth. Darn. I hope I hope. I hope I hope I hope I hope. I hope I won't have to spend so many more nights alone listening to Jewel and Joni Mitchell while staring at the stars up above and wishing and wishing and wishing for love!

Dramatic
James, fifties

*James, an emotionally and physically abusive father,
has a fit during his daughter's wedding rehearsal.*

JAMES: Redemption? For what? For not being nuts? For seeing reality? Huh? Ya'll are the ones who should be begging for forgiveness! Baptizing yourself in a fucking bathtub and spending thousands of dollars on a party?!!? While people outside are starving! People are starving out there!!! Wake up! You think you're close to a higher power but I know more than you. THE HOMELESS KNOW MORE THAN YOU. THE ANIMALS KNOW MORE THAN YOU. THE DUCKS IN THE SKY! AND YET YOU....YOU ALLL...YOU ALL STEP ON THEM! LIKE THEY'RE PIECES OF SHIT. WELL I'M NOT SHIT. I'M NOT SHIT!!! I'M NOT!!!!! ALL OF YOU ARE NUTS! N.U.T.S! NUTS!YOU are all broken AND ROTTEN like the rest of us but ya'll act like ya'll are fixed. Lookin' to JESUS to fix your shit. OPEN YOUR EYES! You're the problem!!! I'm not the problem. YOU'RE THE PROBLEM. I don't expect NO-BODY to do NOTHIN least of all FIX my shit. Because that's lazy! That's right, you're all lazy and you're all nuts and none of you don't know fuck about shit! How about instead of looking for God in a FUCKING man-made building with your head up your ass—try finding god in God in yourself. How about that?! Both of ya'll are gonna learn about life real fucking fast you spoiled pieces of shit! Y'ALL are never gonna be anything. Ya'll gonna be broke. And unhappy. Just like your sister.

Dramatic
Ryan, eighteen

Ryan, a senior in high school and gay and proud, talks to the audience.

RYAN: I think it's really good to live now because you can do what you want to and the kids at my school are cool with you being different than they are. My uncle was talking about the sixties and free love and stuff. It sounded like everyone was trying to be different but ended up being the same. I can wear something weird and at school they'll say, oh, that's like weird, that's so cool. And they think I'm really different, because I'm really different from them, but then I go to New York City to visit my aunt and uncle in Greenwich Village and I walk around with my cousin and it's like I'm not really different at all. Everybody there is even more different than I am. Because I'm living in a time when different is normal. Not like Oscar Wilde and Gertrude Stein and people like that. They were really different. And while it's great to be able to wear what I want, what if I wanted to wear lipstick or nail polish? Would everyone still be cool with me?

Comic
Ted, mid thirties

Ted, an agent, has invited Jimmy, a young actor, to lunch to try and persuade him to dump his current representation and sign with him.

TED: Okay, I'm not going to bullshit you Jimmy. A lot of agents will bullshit you, but I want you to know up front, the last thing that I, Ted Stevens, am is a bullshitter. So I'm going to tell you frankly and honestly why you need to leave your agency and come with me. Jimmy Phillips, I see stardom in you. I see the power to light up a screen, to take possession of an audience, to command a career far surpassing even those of Tom Cruise and Will Smith and Brad Pitt. Now, Jimmy, I'm not going to bullshit you. You got two movies about to be released and one in the can for the spring and right now the buzz about you in this town is sensational. You're hot, hot, hot. Listen, I know the people that represent you now, and Jimmy, I'm not going to bullshit you. For the most part they do an okay job. Unfortunately, all too often, an okay job can take an actor who's hot, hot, hot right back down to cold, cold, cold. So that's why you, Jimmy Phillips, gotta ask yourself, do you want to risk disappearing into oblivion like so many up and coming young actors like yourself have done due to unimaginative, unambitious, uninspired representation? Or do you want to catch that brass ring while you have the chance and become the super star you should be, joining the ranks of Johnny Depp, Matt Damon and...and Ashton Kutcher?

For information on this author, click on the WRITERS tab at www.smithandkraus.com.

Dramatic
Zachary, thirty-five

*It's 2011 in Manhattan. While being fitted for tuxes
for his upcoming nuptials, Zachary begins to feel
some heavy judgment from his Best Man, David. In
an effort to prove that his love for his fiance is real
and everlasting, Zachary takes a fabulous minute
to lay some truth on his commitment-shy Best Man.*

ZACHARY: You want to know something about Jesse?
He never proposed. And neither did I. The night that
Marriage Equality passed, we were at Monster with the
entirety of gay humanity, and I was stifling. I turned to
Jesse and yelled, "I have to get out of here. Equality is
crowding me!" So, we pushed our way through the hip
bones and assholes and finally a projectile *fell* onto the
street, and it was like THERE IT WAS. The night. The
city. The stars, probably. The whole universe just waiting
for us. And out of nowhere, this silly queen just appears
right in front of us, takes us both in his arms and screams,
"Isn't it great?! You two can finally get married! Isn't it
grand!?" And then this stranger, this Christopher Street
Goblin, scampers away, screaming into the night, "Isn't it
great!?" It was such a moment, you know? Like, I could
feel Nora Ephron shining down on us, even though she
still had a few months to live. And I looked at Jesse, and
he looked at me. And we just knew. I'm not marrying him
because it's legal. I'm marrying him because it's love.

For information on this author, click on the
WRITERS tab at www.smithandkraus.com.

Comic
Ian, early twenties

*Ian, awesome gamer, Nevada state champ, has been
recruited by the NSA to operate drones in Iraq and
Afghanistan from a remote bunker in Nevada. The
effects of the violence he's seen through his work
is beginning to bleed into the rest of his life. Here,
he's playing a video war game with an online friend.*

IAN: Look out — there's someone behind that Humvee!

(His friend has nailed the guy.)

Oh, dude! Awesome! He didn't see you coming! Oh crap.
We're surrounded. We're going to need more backup
. . . Wasn't Titan 27 gonna meet us here? Where are
Mongo and Bullet 6? They were supposed to be in this.
What the hell, right? If you say you're gonna show up,
show up. Shit. There's too many of them. I don't think
we can take 'em alone. Ahhh! Frag out! I'm going to
detonate! So listen, dude. You ever wonder, what if this
thing was real? I mean like . . . what if those were actual
people we were blowing up and shit, you know? What
if it weren't soldiers. That you hit. What if . . . Listen.
What if you've got this . . . this building in your cross-
hairs, you've been watching it, you know they're keeping
weapons in there, you've done your surveillance. You've
. . . you've done your job. You know it's a good target.
You get the order, you fire, and just before the missile
hits, like two seconds, this kid, this little girl, looks to be
Addie's age—your sister's age, this . . . this kid walks
around the shed. Out of nowhere. This little girl . . .

*(Something awful happens on the screen. IAN covers his
face which makes them crash. He is shaken, breathing*

hard. He comes back in.)

Ah! Oh fuck man. I'm sorry.

(Pause. He is very shaken.)

Wow, I'm really off tonight. Sorry.

For information on this author, click on the
WRITERS tab at www.smithandkraus.com.

Dramatic
Large, fifteen - seventeen. African American

*Large, a clumsy but overconfident high school stu-
dent, notices Grace, a shy Asian American girl, in
the hallways at school. After a failed first attempt,
he sharpens his approach and finally makes his play
for her by her locker.*

LARGE: C'mon, now! You makin this harder than it has ta
be. *(short beat)* You Chinese, right? I'm juss askin' so I
don't put my foot in my mouth. You are Chinese, aren't
you? *(Pause)* I was thinkin' last night that I fucked up.
I knew I shoulda taken Chinese instead of Spanish.
Couldn't figger out what reason I had for thinkin' that
way, but somethin tol' me I shoulda taken Chinese. I
mean, I know you speak English an' all that - heard you
speak perfect English my damn self —but I wonder if I
was to break out my Chinese to you if my game might
be a l'il tighter right about now. So how's about this:

(Sounds it out crudely, phonetically.)

Wo xian liao jie ni. You unnerstand that? I said that right?
I'm guessin' I did, on account of tha way you lookin at
me. But lemme try again, just in case:

(Again, phonetically sounds it out.)

Wo xian liao jie ni.

(He smiles, a short beat, then:)

You really killin me with this. You know that, don-
chu? You gonna make me say it in English, ain't you? All
the eggrolls I had to eat at the Chinese food place on tha
corner near my house, and you gonna make me say it in
English. Lemme make sure you catch it—in English—so

I don't have to repeat myself again.

(He sighs, then loudly over-articulates the next five words, sounding them out as he had with the Chinese.)

I want to know you.

Comic
Nietzsche, late thirties.

In 1882, Friedrich Nietzsche, the great philosopher, a painfully awkward genius, is hopelessly in love with the beautiful and brilliant Lou Salomé. He has bungled his attempt to propose marriage to her, and admitted that he is terrible at all human relations. Here he describes to her his earlier attempt to propose to a woman, which also did not go very well.

NIETZSCHE: I proposed to Mathilde Trampedach. It was a disaster of operatic proportions. When she walked into the room, I was standing on my head. When I get nervous, I stand on my head. It helps me relax. She was a little taken aback by it, but I decided since she was there, I might as well go through with it, so I asked her for her hand. And I hastened to add that I didn't mean I actually wanted her hand. I didn't want to cut it off and put it in formaldehyde. I meant her hand in marriage. I was making a joke. I suppose it was a joke. But Mathilde just stared at me like a dead fish. But I told myself, I must be strong. I must take charge of the situation. So I got on my knees. Well actually, I fell over, because I'd been standing on my head for a while, and I was a little dizzy, so I thought, well, I'm crawling around on my hands and knees anyway, and it's traditional to propose on one's knees, but she just looked more and more alarmed, as if she thought I was going to start barking like a trained seal, so I told her I had loved her all my life, and she pointed out that I hadn't known her all my life, but I said I'd loved her before I knew her, and even after I knew her, and also while standing on my head, and that I felt closer to her than my mustache, that I loved her more than my mustache, and that in some ways she resembled my mustache, although she didn't actually have a mustache, but her father had a fine mustache, and perhaps some day she would have one, too, or inherit it when he died, I really didn't know what I was saying, it was a desperate attempt to be charming, which obviously I am not, so I told her I wanted to spend the rest of my life with her, which I didn't think was going to be very long anyway, and that if she married me she would no longer be burdened with the hideous name of Trampedach, that she could henceforward be known as Frau Trampedach-Nietzsche, although Nietzsche is also a fairly hideous name, which nobody has ever successfully spelled. And I asked her to please answer soon, because my knees hurt so bad I wasn't sure I could get up. And then it occurred to me that she might be hungry, so I asked her if she wanted a bite of my wienerschnitzel, which I always keep in my pants pocket, and I fear she mistook this for some sort of inappropriate advance, so I begged her to forgive me, since I had been of late much preoccupied with the question of whether, if God is all powerful, he has the power to die? And if he'd want to, because at that point, I certainly did, and that's when she told me she could never marry me because I was just too bizarre, and I got upset and accused her of being terrified of her emotions, and she said, no, she was just terrified of me, and I said, yes, I am very frightening, and screamed BOOGELDY BOOGELDY at her, and she ran away shrieking. Why do all women flee from me? What am I doing wrong?

Seriocomic
Nietzsche, mid forties

Nietzsche, a great philosopher, is slowly going mad.
He has taken to having long, increasingly bizarre
conversations with an audience that exists only in
his head. Here, as his evil sister is preparing to
steal once and for all control of his life's work, he
speaks to his imaginary audience, us, about the
nature of reality, sanity, and ultimately reveals to us
his true and terrible divinity, just before he is struck
by lightning.

NIETZSCHE: Success in the theatre earns my contempt.
Only failure implies good work because in the theatre
there is much loneliness, but no solitude. Or is it the other
way round? I get most things the wrong way round, because it's more interesting that way, except with a horse.
I've been out wandering in thunderstorms, eating grass
like Nebuchadnezzar and Lear. They're playing Wagner
in the square. His music is like the flatulent exhalations of
God's decomposition. Will you stop that damned racket?
I require music, but Wagner makes me vomit. God, on the
other hand, is the author of a play constructed entirely of
darkness and deafening silence, in which he has stationed
professional assassins at all the exits, so that on the way
out, every member of the audience is killed. Perhaps for
some of you it would be a welcome release from the te-
dium of your experience here, or from the horror of your
life in that absurd imaginary world outside. Although to
leave one theatre is to enter another one. And yet from
time to time in the theatre of our suffering there appears
to squirt briefly into being the illusion of ecstasy. And
that is the reason for my present manifestation here, my

bleating little friends. Do you not recognize me? I am the god who has drawn this caricature. I am the face of your demented werewolf lover, come to devour you. Strip naked, eat flesh and die, for I am the god Dionysus. If any other deity has the bad taste to believe he exists, I dare him to strike me down, right here, right now, at this moment.

Seriocomic
Nathan, mid-twenties

*Nathan, furious with his Uncle Bob about the ongo-
ing catastrophes imperiling their family's Minneap-
olis-based carpet cleaning business, demands to be
allowed to rectify the situation, unaware Uncle Bob
has just scratched off a winning lottery ticket.*

NATHAN: Well. Uncle Bob. Guess what? There I was, out
driving in our May blizzard, the backup van wheels
barely staying straight, the steering handle barely holding
steady, the horn going off every time I hit an ice patch,
the largest of which causing me to start heading sideways,
across oncoming traffic until a nice little guard rail saved
me from bounding into lake number ten thousand and
one. Should I wait for a tow? Sorry! Uncle Bob says I
have a schedule to keep. So I hop out of the car to make
sure nothing underneath fell off, when I realize the gear
shift never made it from drive to park. How do I know
this? Because the van is starting to drive away from me.
Yes, the backup van moving along with me standing
there. I start panic running and just barely grasp the rear
panel and haul myself into back storage. I scramble to
the front driver's seat just in time to swerve-avoid slam-
ming into some jackknifed semi-truck road-blocking the
whole freeway. Should I stop and see if anyone needs
help? No time! Uncle Bob says I have a schedule to keep!
Miraculously, the backup van is still drivable, sort of. The
crash only shorted all dashboard electronics. No front
wipers. No heat. So I physically force down the driver
window, and stick my head out the side with a Memorial
Day blizzard firing into my face. I make it to the Showers
house. I lug hardware to the front door. What's that, Mr.

Showers? You don't have a scheduled cleaning? Showers doesn't have a scheduled cleaning. He has a daughter. Her name is April. Her name is April Showers. Did you or did you not conspire with Showers, telling him I was coming to rescue his daughter from her surname? Turns out April's hot. Guess I can't be that furious at you for setting me up with her on your birthday, except my face is thawing and my clothes are ripped and my hair is frozen back and April is scared of my presence and meanwhile this is all happening while we're incurring revenue loss at thirty cents a square foot which means our business continues to lose money and backup vans and backup van electronics by the minute. So this is what I want to tell you. I've been here for five years. Five years ago I decided not to go to college. Five years ago against my dead father's wishes I came into the family business. To help Aunt Agnes. And you. And for five years I've taken no vacation, no sick, nothing. Work all day and sleep on the floor in back at night. For five years. I haven't seen an April Showers or even a May blizzard because this is all I've had. And now I want what you said. What you said. A stake in the business. A real stake, as partners, okay? How's that for direct and honest? And I'm fine, thanks for asking.

For information on this author, click on the WRITERS tab at www.smithandkraus.com.

Comic
Wendell, mid-forties

*Wendell Sash, a salesman in his mid-forties, demon-
strates to John Haskell, a rich, skeptical banker in
his early sixties, why he is considered one of the best
decorative driveway salesmen in the world.*

WENDELL: Fundamentally, what I use is a three step process, although I very seldom need to use the third step.
In the first step I appeal to your sense of the esthetic. I
point out how much warmer and inviting a decorative
driveway would make your home look. Just as a curios-
ity, what sort of house do you live in John? You'll most
likely remain perfectly satisfied with it as long as you
don't think about something else. Like an awesome,
elegant, matching red brick, circular driveway. An awesome, elegant, matching red brick, circular driveway
that would turn that very fine, solid, two story redbrick
house of yours into a much more eye catching and breath
taking structure than it already is. Now I go to step two
and produce documentation proving that if you did put
in this awesome, elegant, matching red brick, circular
driveway, almost immediately the value of your very
fine, solid, two story redbrick house increases by twice
what that awesome, elegant, matching red brick, circular
driveway cost. And then with inflation being what it is,
well, figure it out John. By not putting in this awesome,
elegant, matching red brick, circular driveway, you will
actually be losing money. Well, John, in the third and
final step I appeal to your great pride in being who you
are. Your ego, your vanity and the rapture of being you. I
point out the fact that every time you look out your front

window at that awesome, elegant, matching red brick, circular driveway, that incredibly stunning, impressive, awesome, elegant, matching redbrick, circular driveway that both you and I know, you don't really want. You don't really need. That majestic, outrageously over-priced, self indulgent, elegant, awesome, matching red brick, circular driveway, that frankly, only a very select few can afford, will be saying, not just to you, to your neighbors, to your business associates, to your mailman, to your gardener, to your friends as well as your enemies, to every living man, woman and child who sees it, drives by it, walks near to it . . . . It will be saying "Hey, look at me America. My name is John Haskell and like it or not, I've got the world by the balls!

For information on this author, click on the WRITERS tab at www.smithandkraus.com.

Seriocomic
Len, forties-fifties, multiracial

Len, a war veteran and presidential candidate whose ethnic make-up contains every race on earth, speaks to his Republican operative handler in a reflective moment. He may also be a serial killer.

LEN: Having every culture inside me gets pretty overwhelming sometimes. It's like . . . You know when you walk into an Irish bar and you're like: wow this feels like home. But then you're not really Irish but I mean I am but I've never actually been to Ireland? I also have trace memories of Egypt. You know, pharaohs, the Nile, those drawings with the people turned sideways? I somehow have those images inside me too. Who am I. That is the question. I've been to China. I returned to America and cried. I wanted to stay out there. In the swarms of people, who were moving and living and I didn't mean a thing to them. I was at home in my invisibility. In America I was too much inside and outside myself at the same time. I wanted to keep moving did not want to stand still and have a culture encrust around me. I wanted back into the swarms of China. I was myself there in the wilderness of others who were still my blood yes moving through the wilderness of my blood felt so right. And I breathed the air in deeply. And I coughed because the air in China is terrible. And I drank China tea and though it might have been the same imported tea I drank in America in China I *tasted China* because I had become a vessel for experience. And I felt the same thing in Afghanistan felt I could start a life there because I had emptied myself and was ready for a new form. But of course it was impossible I knew I had to leave or this Afghani culture would stick to me and I would lose me in the same way I lost me in America. And of course in Afghanistan I killed lots of locals so that definitely helped ebb any preemptive homesickness because nothing ebbs homesickness like killing your relatives so yeah that helped killing Afghanis definitely helped.

For information on this author, click on the WRITERS tab at www.smithandkraus.com.

Dramatic
Mark, late thirties-late forties

Mark excoriates his new neighbor Steven after he overhears him mock him through the thin walls. This is after Steven and his girlfriend look up Mark online and have a field day making fun of him. It's a clash between generations in tight New York City quarters.

MARK: I know you have everything. You're smart and you've had more than a modicum of success. You have a dominant personality so you're used to people giving you what you want. You can go to Los Angeles and attend fancy art openings and mingle with beautiful people who will listen to you and if that doesn't work out, then you can fall back on your old job or your parents for that matter. You have thousands of friends and followers who actually care what you're up to. We live in the exact same size apartments and I can barely afford mine while yours is a fall back. A fall back. You have no respect or any critical comprehension for what art is. You're an egotistical narcissist who has everything thrust upon you in life and you're not only corrupting your girlfriend's art, but you have no regard or respect for the role of art in society. It's all a talent contest to you. It's not about self-reflection. You have no idea what it is to actually struggle or reflect. You slow down digital images? What kind of bullshit is that? Where are *you* in that? And you *mock m*e and my work and corrupt it for others and spread hateful thoughts and guess what? Those hateful thoughts come back to get you. You're a savage. And the only way to deal with savages is to be a savage. I came from nothing. My parents worked in *box factories*. That's all anyone ever talked about, were box factories! I was the faggot with a sister with a deformed limb. You don't know what I've sacrificed! You have NO IDEA what I've lost! And yet you mock me? Without even reading my story? Which — for the record — was the first *honest thing I've ever written.*

For information on this author, click on the WRITERS tab at www.smithandkraus.com.

Comic
Uncle Jim, sixty-three

Uncle Jim has come to Nashville for his nephew Justin's wedding. Justin is a country music star. Here, he is alone in Justin's hotel room. He addresses a blow-up sex doll, whom he calls Wanda June.

UNCLE JIM: Do not waste thy piteous gaze on me, Wanda June. For the man you see before you is not the man I am. And most assuredly, not the man I was. *(Pause)* Man I was stood tall and upright, pillar strong and confident. His boyish face framed by long golden tresses, that smelled of youthful exuberance and Pert Plus Shampoo and Conditioner. Man I was had a beautiful, bright-white smile, conveyin' confidence, ambition and a future filled with possibilities. Possibly. Possible. Pumpkin pie. *(Pause)* Man I had eyes the bluest of blue, that sparkled in the sun and viewed the world as a joyous, wondrous playground, filled with all the promises of God. *(Pause)* But, shit happens, my dear. Twenties give way to thirties, thirties blend into your forties, forties melt into fifties and the rest is just a series of five year blinks all the way to the fuckin' grave. The once lustrous hair has now vanished. Replaced by a dry, barren, near-dead scalp. The pearly smile is now a mouth full of chipped, cracked, yellowbrown bitin' bones. Stained from years of instant coffee, filter-less cigarettes and swallowin' the shit of a thousand lesser men. And the eyes, once sparklin' with dreams have now faded. Milked over by a lifetime of heartache, struggle and plain old rotten luck. *(Pause)* I apologize, Wanda June. Afraid I'm not very good company this evening *(Pause)* Old bull and a young bull, standin' top of a hill, pasture below is filled with beautiful, grazin' dairy cows. *(He crosses to the couch, sits, sighs, then puts the gun on the floor, the barrel aimed at his head)* UNCLE JIM Young bull says, "Let's run down there and fuck seven or eight of them cows." Old bull says "No, let's walk down . . . and fuck' em all." *(Pause)* Fuck them all.

For information on this author, click on the WRITERS tab at www.smithandkraus.com.

Dramatic
Ben, thirty-one

*Ben explains to Barbra the horror of the oncoming
zombies.*

BEN: This room looks pretty secure. If we have to, we can run in here and board up the doors. It won't be long before those things are back pounding their way in here. They're afraid now. They're afraid of fire. I've found that out. You know that place back down the road called Beatman's? Beatman's Diner? Anyhow, that's how I found that truck I have out there. There's a radio in the truck. I had jumped in to listen to it when a big gasoline truck came screaming right across the road with—there must have been ten, fifteen of those things chasing after it, grabbing and holding on. Now, I didn't see them at first. I could just see that the truck was moving in a funny way and those things were catching up to it. The truck went right across the road. I slammed on my breaks to keep from hitting it myself. It went right through the guardrail. I guess-I guess the driver must have cut off the road into that gas station by Beatman's Diner. It went right through the billboard. It went right through the gas pump and never stopped moving. By now it's like a moving bonfire. I didn't know if the truck was going to explode or what. I can still hear the man, screaming. This thing is just backing away from it. I looked back at the diner to see if there was anyone there who could help me. That's when I noticed that the entire place had been encircled. There wasn't a sign of life left, except . . . By now there were no more screams. I realized that . . . I was alone with fifty or sixty of those things just standing there staring at me. I-I started to drive. I just plowed right through them. They didn't move. They didn't run or—They just stood there staring at me. I just wanted to crush them. And they . . . scattered through the air like bugs.

For information on this author, click on the WRITERS tab at www.smithandkraus.com.

Dramatic
Adam, sixteen

When Adam was 10, he accidentally shot and killed his 9-year-old brother Joey. His mother had taken the ammunition clip out of the gun, so he thought it was not loaded. He is talking to a social worker who has come to interview his family to see if Adam can be released from parole.

ADAM: I know two families from the inside out. The one I was born into. And the one I destroyed. *(beat)* So, um, anyway. We're laughing and then Joey sort of flops over the chair —right where you're sitting actually, and then that's when I remember, oh yeah, the gun's in the cabinet. So I pull it out. And - at first I pointed it at the door and I closed my eye just like my dad taught me to when we went hunting —and I *pretended* to pull the trigger. I made that sound like "pow." And then I brought it a little closer—maybe at the picture on the wall, I don't really remember, and I did it again— just like fake pulled the trigger and said "pow." And then the last time I pointed it right at him— just like we were hunting—and I looked at Joey and he was laughing with his blue tongue and I just . . . I pulled the trigger. For real. And it went off. I shot him right in the head. Didn't miss or anything. I mean I wasn't far but still—sometimes you miss. Because the thing I didn't know was that when you take the clip off of a gun like that -there's still one bullet that's up in the chamber. I didn't mean to hurt him. I didn't mean to ruin everything. I was only playing. I just—I'm sorry. Please. Tell them . . . just tell them all I'm sorry.

For information on this author, click on the WRITERS tab at www.smithandkraus.com.

Dramatic
Thomas, thirties

Kim, Thomas' girlfriend, has put a hiatus on their relationship because she needs some space," but actually she fears that "the other thing" which sometimes takes her over will kill him. Thomas has come back to her to plead with her to allow them to get back together. He doesn't know about her murderous doppelganger; all he knows is that she fears that something terrible will happen.

THOMAS: When I was a kid, my sister was like my favorite person on earth because she was funny and cool and she would buy me things all the time—candy, toys, comic books. One time she got me this robot thing that turned into a dinosaur because I had asked for one for my birthday but my folks didn't have the money and they got me a little plastic dinosaur thing instead because it was cheaper. I've told you about this. You know how she was. But here's something I didn't tell you. You know why she left? Because one day, she showed up after school to pick me up. Like, as a treat, because she knew I hated taking the bus home. And she gets there and she's out of her mind high on whatever it was back then, and I didn't really know what was going on with her but I knew she was acting weird and her eyes were all funny and I said I didn't want to get in the car with her. And she got really upset. And she started crying and telling me, "Get in the car! Thomas, get in the car!" And someone from the school saw and came over all "What's going on? What's the problem?" And she's like, I'm his sister. Tell them, Tell them." And. I didn't say anything. I was silent, while she's crying and pleading. And this teacher or whoever it was, he's like, "I'm going to call the police," and that scares her, so she peels out of there and drives off, and he says "is everything okay? Are you okay?" And I'm like, "Yeah, I'm fine." And I get on the bus and go home, and that night I find out that she totaled the car driving around town and my parents kicked her out of the house and we didn't see her for two years. And that fucked me up for a while, because I was like, I should've just gotten in the car, I should've just gotten in the car and said she was my sister and we would have driven home and it would have been fine. But I didn't tell them she was my sister 'cause I was ashamed of her and I was scared and then I didn't see her for two years. But that's not my fault. That's what I know now. And it doesn't matter if I would have done things different because it wouldn't have changed how she is. *(beat)* Terrible things happen. And everything isn't always your fault.

Dramatic
Carl, late fifties

Carl, a ghost hunter, is being interviewed by a journalist, who has asked him about his clients.

CARL: You were asking about. About what kinda people call us up. And I reckon most of the time, it's women like Mrs. Kelly here. They don't really know who to turn to. Widowed or. Or living alone. Or if it's a married couple, nine times out of ten it's the wife calls us up, asking about. About what we can do for 'em. Go figure. So, when we're dealing with, ah. With a woman like Mrs. Kelly. And say she's got a real bad haunting on her hands. We gotta tell her about it in a way she can handle it. You know: "Yes, there's a spirit out here. We picked up some disturbances. There's, ah, there's reason to believe you got a haunting here." But you don't got to tell 'em all the details, not all at once. Cause there ain't too much you can do about it when you know. If you're talking about getting rid of the ghosts or—See, most of the time ghosts don't respond too well to that sort of thing. The dead don't like to be disturbed. They like to be the ones doing the disturbing. A lot of times the best thing to do is just let them be. Let them know that you hear them, that you see them, and then let them be. People think about ghosts like they're these all-powerful, all-knowing beings. But they aren't, really. They were people themselves once, like you and me. And the longer they're stuck in this world, the angrier they get. They get angry and bored and frustrated, and over time, they're gonna start lashing out at the people around them. At the people they used to love, sometimes. *(beat)* I was watching a TV show once—long before I started up the business here—and there was a guy on the program, a psychic kind of a guy, and he was talking to a woman been haunted by her dead sister something like three decades. And she never had a problem with it before, because it was never a problem before, Gave her a kind of comfort, actually, or that's what she said. Then one day, and she didn't know why, the spirit just turned on her. She felt a hand push her down a flight of stairs, ended up in the emergency wing with a concussion and 17 stitches in her head. And she knew it was her sister, even though she didn't know why she'd, you know' Why she'd turn on her like that, all of a sudden. *(beat)* Psychic tried to talk to the dead sister, but I dunno if it worked. He wasn't the, ah. The real deal. I know the real deal when I see it, and he ain't it. *(beat)* And maybe she was just a crackpot anyway— people trip going down the stairs all the time. Single woman, living alone at her age. You know what those women are like.

PARIS AT DAWN
Eric Grant

Dramatic
François, thirty, French

François, a Parisian history professor and painter,
tells an American neighbor why music is even more
important to him than art.

FRANÇOIS: I thank God every day for being a painter. But
music . . . I wish I could write music. Music is the highest
art. Nothing can take your breath away like music. Nothing in the world can transport you to higher places than a
good song. Music is like falling in love with someone. All
your life you hear different songs all day long, yes? Some
of them linger for a few days, perhaps even a few months.
Some are catchy, and some may make you a little happy
for a while. Then one day you hear a piece of music . . .
Perhaps you had heard it before but didn't realize it . . .
Or perhaps you've heard it all your life but never really
listened, until this one special moment when it hits you in
the face . . . You find one astounding piece of music that
fills your heart with . . . For example, when I moved to
Paris originally, I hated it. I hated everybody in it, and I
couldn't understand why people loved it so much. I was
so lonely. I hated all the guys here. I had been cheated
on three times by the same man . . . One weekend my
friends convinced me to go to the symphony. I did not
understand why, because I did not like the symphony!
They played some music that I already heard before, it
was nothing very special . . . At the end, there was this
movement from a symphony of, ah, Rachmaninov . . . It
begins very simple. On paper it sounds like it should be
so boring. The melody just repeated every few minutes
like a chorus of a bad pop song. And it goes on for fifteen minutes! But it's not boring at all. It's the complex

idea of love. How love changes throughout our lives. Because every time the melody was brought back, the context changed. It represented important moments of love in our lives. Birth, first love, first kiss, the love of your family . . . Then the love you miss when it is finally taken away. Accepting the beauty and love in death. *(Pause)* Toward the end, there is a subtle build-up. Yes? Build-up? A subtle build-up and all of a sudden the entire orchestra crescendos and plays the melody together as one single being. And I felt this . . . this awakening! A sense of this something inside of me bursting. I had never felt anything like it. I felt myself being carried . . . lifted up to another world. Heaven. I felt Heaven. Like when you wake up at the end of winter, and the air smells of spring. Like Paris at dawn.

For information on this author, click on the WRITERS tab at www.smithandkraus.com.

Paul Lewis

Dramatic
Hal, thirties-forties

Hal is a married father in his 30s to 40s. Several weeks previously he was sitting in a minor league baseball park with his eight-year-old son when a foul-ball line drive just outside the first base line struck and killed the boy. Now the rookie shortstop who hit the ball, Bobby Sinclair, has shown up unannounced at Hal and Elaine's house, filled with remorse. Hal is the very picture of sullen silence until, quite suddenly, he feels compelled to speak.

HAL: Bobby. Listen to me. As of right now, as of this very night, you have to stop thinking about that night at the ballpark, about the what-ifs and what-might-have-beens. That's all in the past now. You can't go through life second-guessing yourself because you decided to swing for the fences. A mistake like that: it may have been a minor strategic error. But it wasn't a mistake of the heart. Now, a father's job . . . part of a father's job is to protect his son from foul balls and other deadly projectiles. To put himself between a line drive and his son. That was my job. And the truth is, I didn't do my job. Didn't keep my end of the bargain. Now, that was a mistake of the heart. *(a beat)* Don't interrupt me, now. Just hear me out. The distance between home plate and the mound is sixty feet, six inches. We were easily two, maybe two-and-a-half times that distance away. That's a hundred-and-fifty feet, give or take a few. If that ball was going, say, eighty miles an hour, I had nearly two seconds to react. And this is what I can't accept. When you're a father, you take that second, or that two seconds, and you do whatever is necessary, don't you think, Bobby? I mean, you hear

---

stories all the time, about dads lifting cars off their children, feats of superhuman strength— *(a beat)* No, let me finish. Because I'm trying to understand it. And no excuses, no amount of rationalization is going to bring me any closer to an understanding. I ask myself: how did I let it happen? And I'll be searching for the answer to that question for the rest of my life.

For information on this author, click on the WRITERS tab at www.smithandkraus.com.

Dramatic
The President, sixty-one

In the year 1974, on the eve of his resignation, the President of the United States sits in the White House late at night, drinking, and talking with a very nervous and uncomfortable Secret Service agent. The President has had too much to drink, and has been contemplating a number of desperate measures. He is bitter, defiant, and, part of him, ashamed.

THE PRESIDENT: They killed Jack Kennedy. That handsome, smooth talking, horny, smug son of a bitch. Everything was so fucking easy for him. Women. Politics. Football. Everything that was hard for me was easy for him. Money. His fucking crook of a father stole the fucking election in Chicago. Camelot. Shit. Do you know he was once my friend? It's true. When we were in Congress together. He was my friend. When Jack Kennedy walked into the room suddenly it was like I was the fucking wallpaper. God, how I hated him. Do you know who killed him? You think you know who killed him, but you don't know anything. That cocksucker Hoover knew. But you don't want to know. Because that's how this country is really run. In the dark. In the fucking dark. All of them have done it that way. All of them. But me, me, they want to impeach. The dirty fuckers. You want to know who really runs America, sonny? You don't want to know. If you knew, you'd never sleep again. I haven't had a good night's sleep since 1947. Maybe I've never had a good night's sleep. Do you think I don't know? Do you think I'm stupid? Do you think I don't see that you're all conspiring against me? Last night I was walking, all through this place, in the dark, talking to the paintings.

I had a lovely conversation with George Washington. George Washington was six feet four inches tall, and his wife was the size of a small dog. Can you imagine those two going at it? Did he take his wooden teeth out, do you think? And I said to him, George, George, look what they've done to your fucking country. What am I supposed to do? And do you know what the Father of His Country said to me? Do you know what he said? He said, Dick, you need a shave.

Dramatic
The President, sixty-one

*Late at night, in the year 1974, the President of the
United States has been up all night drinking and
talking to an increasingly uneasy Secret Service
man. Among the recurring obsessions that haunt
him are his hatred for the easy charm, good looks
and confidence of John Kennedy, the dark secrets
he believes he knows about where power really lies
in America, and also the memory of the last time he
was completely happy, sitting on a porch in the rain
as a boy and reading Sherlock Holmes stories. He is
fascinated by the moment when Holmes and Moriarty
go over Reichenbach Falls in a mortal embrace, and
only Holmes returns. He is really talking about the
baffling juxtaposition of good and evil in his own
soul. The bastards he's referring to are privileged
Eastern Ivy League types, who are born into a sense
of entitlement and power.*

THE PRESIDENT: I always hated those bastards. The ones
who thought they were better than me. But what you
don't understand until it's too late is that step by step,
you become them. You become the enemy. You become
what you hate the most. But even then, you're still not
a member of the club. You'll never be a member of the
club. I know I'm incoherent. I've had strange experiences. Experiences you wouldn't believe. Because the
story we tell about ourselves is an absolute perversion
of the facts. The real truth is too horrible for anybody to
know. He took up beekeeping. After he got done taking
violin lessons in Tibet. Have you read the Tibetan Book
of the Dead? Everything is made of ghosts. Tonight I

thought I saw something scrambling over the garden wall. I can feel the haunting in this house. Something is waiting, like a spider at the center of its web. Something reptilian. Moriarty had hereditary tendencies of the most diabolical kind. Jekyll left. Hyde came back. Holmes left. Moriarty came back. But here's the thing. They're the same person. They were always the same person. The man whose daughters love and respect him, and the man who sits in his office planning criminal activities. They're the same person. Let me give you some advice, son. Get the hell out of here. Run as fast as you can away from this place and never come back.

(Pause.)

It's almost morning. It's the last morning in the history of the world. Time to fall on the grenade. Go home and make love to your wife. The thing is, I'm going over the falls today. Too bad I never learned to swim.

Dramatic
Phil, late thirties

*Phil is a local dogcatcher in Brighton, an English
seaside town. He is talking to his younger brother
Bertie, who is now living with Phil after having
spent many years in and out of various institutions
and several suicide attempts. They are living in the
house they grew up in. Their mother now has a flat
in Eastbourne, using money from their father's life
insurance. Bertie stutters, and doesn't have his shot
together. Phil takes the responsibility of having to
look after him, as well as running the house very
seriously, and he is always looking for ways to try
and improve their financial outlook. Here, Phil is
trying to engage Bertie in a discussion as they have
breakfast together. Phil, more than anything, wants
Bertie to be 'normal.'*

PHIL: Look at this. They found another one. 23 years
old. Strangled. Mutilated. Cuts all over. They reckon he
dragged her body through some bushes after he killed
her, mile or two, before dumping her on the tracks. Same
stretch as before and all. The Moulescombe line. It's a
pattern, innit? Now why do you think he does that? Why
d'you think this bastard drags them through the woods
after he's killed 'em? He picks these remote spots to do
the deed, right? Then he drags 'em a mile, two miles
through bushes and bracken or whatnot, and dumps 'em
by the tracks. He could just as easily dig a shallow grave
right where he is. Why go to all the hassle? The risk if being seen? I'll tell you why: Because he wants them to be
found. Wants people to know what he's done. Proud of it
he is. It's craftwork. Wood-whittling or whathaveyou. All

those tiny cuts. Thinks of himself as an artist. Part of him probably actually *wants* to get caught. Wants everyone to know *who* he is, how smart he is. Get his name in the papers. History's Greatest Serial Killers, that sort of thing. I mean he knows as well as anyone the cops can't catch a cold in winter, right? That's why he dumps 'em on the rail tracks. He's taunting them. Gives him a feeling of superiority. Coz the truth about this psycho is: he's a nobody. I guarantee you - this bloke – you wouldn't look twice at him on the High Street. Sugar. Regular looking as anyone else. You might have bumped into him at the shops this morning. How would you know? That's the point I'm making. That's how he's getting away with it. Could be anyone. Could be you for all I know. You could be slicing up all sorts of people. Tossing them on the train tracks. How do I know anything you get up to during the days?

For information on this author, click on the WRITERS tab at www.smithandkraus.com.

Dramatic
McManus, forties, British

*McManus is intelligent, shrewd, well-dressed, elo-
quent. A con-man in the dog fighting game.He is
talking to Bertie, the brother of his 'mark'.*

McMANUS: You know what I think? I think we could become mates, the two of us. Go see a film or something.
Mind you, I've got a lovely collection of British War
Films at my place. Perhaps you could come over some
time and we can watch them together. Make some pop-
corn. I'm quite amusing once you get to know me. *(slight
pause)* No I've never understood the appeal of Seaside
towns. Inflatable crocodiles, the smell of seaweed and
sun-tan lotion. Tourists. But it's the damp I really can't
abide. The way it seeps into your bones. The buildings.
This house is probably full of it. Dry rot, wet rot. Mold. I
read a fascinating article the other day, in The Telegraph,
about the effects of mold on the human body: Lung dis-
ease. Rashes. Nausea. Infections. Senility. Senility. It's
the mycotoxins you see. Breathing them in day after day.
People are getting sick and going mad by doing nothing more but living in their own homes. All these years
they've been thinking senility might be genetic, turns
out it's in the walls. Extraordinary. Take my word for it:
have this place inspected before it's too late.

For information on this author, click on the
WRITERS tab at www.smithandkraus.com.

Dramatic
McManus, forties. British.

McManus is intelligent, shrewd, well-dressed, elo-
quent. A con-man in the dog fighting game. He has
tied Bertie to a chair and is wiring an electrical
circuit to administer shocks to him, as a means of
extorting money from Bertie's brother, Phil.

McMANUS: I'm going to take a wild stab in the dark and
assume you've never heard of a man by the name of
Phalaris. Mildly erotic moniker I admit, but we all have
our cross to bear. Anyway this Phaliris chappie was a
tyrant in Ancient Sicily - 500 years before the birth of
Our Lord and Saviour, if you're to believe such hocus-
pocus—and he had a marvelous reputation for excessive
cruelty. Granted, instilling fear in as many people as
possible is the prerequisite for successful tyranny, but
Phalaris was a master at it. Rumour has it he engaged
in cannibalism with a taste suckling babies. I take that
with a pinch of salt. If you'll forgive the imagery. But
one thing we do know about Phalaris—one thing we are
absolutely certain on—is his invention of The Brazen
Bull. The Brazen Bull was an immaculately crafted piece
of workmanship by all accounts. All brass. Hollow on
the inside. This thing was big enough to fit 7 or 8 men in.
Little trap door on one side. And what Phalaris did was:
he put his enemies—or, I suppose, pretty much anyone
he fancied - inside the stomach of this brass bull. And he
lit a fire underneath. The whole creature turned into a human oven. Naturally this resulted in an inordinate amount
of screaming from the poor souls inside as they slowly
roasted to death. But the ingenious part, the part that
makes Phalaris such an endless source of fascination was
that he built into this torture device an elaborate series of

tubes and stops. So the screams of his roasting enemies were forced out through the nostrils of the creature in such a way that it resembled the sound of an angry bull. You can imagine how popular it became. People would travel for miles to hear The Brazen Bull snorting away. You see what good old Phalaris managed to do was turn ordinary torture into Performance Art. Quick test of the voltage meter. Don't worry, I'm not going to burn you alive like old Phalaris—You're not my enemy, Bertie. It's your brother that has wronged me. He's indebted to me. Financially, and, quite frankly, personally. You see I'm here to collect what he owes me. You're merely here to provide the motivation. Now then—How about we take your gag off?

For information on this author, click on the WRITERS tab at www.smithandkraus.com.

Dramatic
Tom, thirties

*Tom is speaking to his wife, Jen. It's the middle of
the night and Tom's explaining why he can't sleep.
Jen is pregnant and dying. Western medicine offers
her no hope. Against Tom's better judgement, she's
got a meeting in the morning with Romeo Chang,
an Eastern medicine healer she hopes will keep her
alive long enough to have her baby.*

TOM: I got fixated on Iran. About those diplomatic talks we're – you know, their weapons . . . underground tunnels . . . Who are we to even say who can blow up the world and who can't? That's what I was thinking about. And . . . you. And the president. Everything that must keep him up at night. About maudlin shit that doesn't seem so maudlin in the context of a new life. About humming birds showing up in March. About those bugs in Colorado that are killing all the trees because the winter's too warm to hibernate. We need those trees. Every last one . . . to give off oxygen so we can breathe. I'm suffocating in the dark. How can anyone with children let the world go to shit? How do I do this without you? How do I do anything without you? That's what I was thinking about . . . About being alone . . . about all the decisions . . . . by my-(self) . . . .with your fath-(er) . . . .how do I keep from (killing him)? . . . about first days of school and new lunch boxes and clean little ruffled ankle sox and fresh-smelling sneakers. And about how happy we should be. About all the extra packaging on my headphones and the plastic that isn't recyclable. About the number "four" and "five" plastic containers we get from China Kitchen when we can only recycle "one" and "two." About jerking off in the shower to fantasies of *you* now . . . my unattainable wife. I'm not talking about sex. I really don't know how to reach you sometimes. I'm already missing you. I hate myself for that. Before we got married, we said we'd go to Turkey or China or Greece or Amsterdam. I really want to get high with you in Amsterdam. I'd really like to get high right now. Then, I could sleep. When did we stop buying pot? When did we do that? That's a very important household staple. From now on, I'm gonna tell China Kitchen: Put it all in paper containers. Save the earth one Chinese food order at a time. And I'm gonna buy some pot. And I guess ultimately, yeah, I'm up cuz I'm thinking about you, and I can't believe a guy with the name Romeo Chang has everything I love in his hands.

For information on this author, click on the WRITERS tab at www.smithandkraus.com.

Dramatic
Romeo Chang, thirties-fifties, could be any ethnicity,
but probably Chinese

Romeo Chang, a washed-up Eastern medicine mas-
ter, is explaining to Jen how he lost his mojo and can't
help her. She's pregnant and dying and out of medical
options. She's heard miraculous stories about him
saving a dying dog and wants him to keep her alive
long enough to have her baby.

ROMEO: I was raised by a lunatic qi-gong master . . . found
me . . . back roads of China . . . . by a river . . . . or a dump-
ster . . . . who knows? Story keeps . . . My mother. I don't
know what she was. Some ex-pat Chinese-o-phile? Military maybe? French? British? A Turk? Maybe she was
16. Maybe it was an affair. Or sex trade. All I know is she
didn't want me. Left me to die . . . . Some days I wished
I had. He was a madman. Made me train harder cuz I
didn't fit in. Like you name a kid Romeo in China, that's
gonna . . . .? Maybe he was a theatre buff. All I know . . .
square peg, round hole, damned from the start. He made
me drink snake venom and whale sperm to test me . . .
eat a pig's uterus . . . It did NOT taste like chicken, by the
way. Anything to please him, which was impossible. It
was a beagle. Stumpy little legs. He could've lived on his
three good ones. But he was Mindy Copenhauer's one
true love. Her soul mate. If they cut off his leg, it was
like cutting off hers. She watches the video . . . calls
. . . . I can hear it through the phone: she's gorgeous . .
. . and rich . . . agrees to $320 a session without blink-
ing. The old man's spirit was pissed! True masters don't
gouge their clients. But then he told every God damn
day from the grave I wasn't a true master. Mindy had

bucks and a bod, and I was gonna take advantage of both. I said yes, and she wrapped her legs around me like a boa constrictor. I was invincible. But a straw through a table does not a healthy dog make. I was with that dog day and night. Months. Maybe years. Meditating. Praying. Fasting. Even when he wasn't with me, he was with me . . . . . seeping through my clothes, my skin, into my heart. Ghost of the old man haunting me every step of the way."A dog!," he'd shriek. "You're killing yourself for a dog?" A true master gets *stronger*—not *weaker*—when he works. And on top of everything else . . . you know what that mutt did after I saved its miserable life? Stole Mindy away from me. The two of 'em walked out on me, six functioning legs between 'em.

For information on this author, click on the WRITERS tab at www.smithandkraus.com.

Dramatic
Eric, forties

Having weaseled out of an earlier deadline by lying to his employer that his wife was pregnant, Eric, an illustrator, now attempts re-negotiate his contract over the phone. But when faced with his impotence in the negotiation, Eric goes for an even bigger, more absurd, and darker lie.

ERIC: Come on. Did you ever think when you handed me that half-assed outline, which I fleshed out for you, *as a favor* . . . I know the contract was clear. Actually, no, you know what? I don't think I even bothered to read the contract because who would have thought that some book about magic bicycles would even get published, and now you're Doctor Fucking Seuss. There's nothing wrong with that. But if you asked anyone in our class who was going to be Doctor Fucking Seuss . . . You do have talent. Clearly you have a talent. But can you just say that Eric does, too? That I also have a talent, and that rewarding me for that talent shouldn't be some outlandish suggestion that sends you into a tailspin. Like if you admit that I contribute something here, that I'm *worth* something . . . I'm out of line. Pause) This isn't your fault. This actually has nothing to do with you. If I could just report back to Melissa that I'm getting a bonus on this one, that would be helpful. *(Pause)* Can I ask you something, Joe? Did you say anything to Melissa about that, about the kid thing? You didn't send her an email? Because remember how I told you not to say anything to her and then—Look, I know that you sent her an email. Are you going to pretend you have no idea what I'm talking about? Yeah, "Congrats." And you know what happened after you sent your congrats? Melissa had a miscarriage. She got your email, which I told you not to, but you don't give a fuck about anything I say, and she freaked out and she started bleeding and we lost the baby, and it's all your fucking fault. So you can shove your favors and your magic bicycles up your ass. Congrats to you, too.

For information on this author, click on the WRITERS tab at www.smithandkraus.com.

Dramatic

Fyodor, twenties (but could be any age)

Fyodor, a hot-headed husband, has visited a gun store in search of the perfect weapon to kill his wife, her lover and himself. There, he encounters a persnickety clerk who challenges him at every turn.

FYODOR: I know what I have to do, so don't try to talk me out of it. Don't you dare! My home is destroyed. My honor is trampled in the mud. Vice is triumphant, but not for long. I have it all worked out. I'll kill her first, then her lover, then myself. I can see it now. Blood-stained corpses. Broken skulls. Oozing brains. The commotion. The gaping spectators. The post-mortem. Ah, the beauty, the justice of it all! It's a pity I won't be around to enjoy it. But you know what? They won't, either. The only question is how I'll do it. That's why I've come to Schmuck & Co., gunsmiths and gun merchants extraordinaire. *(LONG PAUSE)* Why don't I challenge that scoundrel to a duel? This nifty dueling pistol would do the job all right. But, wait, maybe that's doing him too much honor. Beasts like that should be shot in the face at close range, like junkyards dogs. This pistol would blow out their brains. No question. Blood would gush over the carpet and the parquet. My strumpet of a wife – ha! – would twist and turn and cry out in agony and then be heard no more. Ah, the blood, the wailing, the horror of it all! But wait! That's not terrible enough. I have a better idea. I'll kill him. Then I'll kill myself. But I'll spare the Whore of Babylon. Why not? Let her feels the stings of conscience, the world's contempt. For a pretentious soul like hers, that would be worse than death itself. Oh, I can see it now! I, the injured husband, at my own funeral, lying in my coffin with a gentle smile on my lips. And she, the Whore of Babylon, pale, wracked with remorse, following the coffin, not knowing where she can hide to escape the hatred spewed on her like cascading vomit by the mob. Oh, yes! Dogs pee on her. Children spit on her. Old women lean out their windows to empty their chamber pots on her head. *(Pause)* But no! Why should I be dead? Why shouldn't I witness the agonies of the Whore of Babylon? What good is revenge if I'm dead? Revenge is only sweet if I can taste its fruits. Why should I be the one lying there in my coffin, cold as a sturgeon, knowing nothing about it? I'll kill him, then I'll go to his funeral and look on. Then after the funeral, I'll kill myself. They'd arrest me, though, before the funeral, and take away my pistol. Now let me get this straight. I'll kill him. She'll remain alive. For the time being, I'll spare myself and get arrested instead. I'll always have time to kill myself. I can take my sweet time about it. Then, at the preliminary investigation, I'll be able to expose all the infamy of her conduct. You see, if I kill myself and she's still alive, she may, with her usual duplicity and impudence, blame me. Then society will justify her behavior and laugh at me. Besides, why should I kill myself? Suicide is cowardly. So I'll kill him and let her live. I'll face my trial. Yes, I'll endure my trial, and she will be brought into court as a witness. I can see it now. Surely, the court, the press, the public – all will sympathize with me.

For information on this author, click on the WRITERS tab at www.smithandkraus.com.

Dramatic
Reggie, thirties, African American

*Reggie is a foreman in a stamping plant that is on
the ropes, laying off workers. Here, he tells Faye, a
co-worker, that he finally snapped under the pressure
and attacked his supervisor.*

REGGIE: It was the way he said it that really made me—I
just couldn't listen to him talkin' like that. Couldn't let
him. Spoke about you like you wasn't even—like you
wasn't Faye. Like you had no name or no—history or
no—"Dead weight" he say—just like that—like you
wasn't even—I just couldn't let him. I felt it in my chest.
Like dynamite burstin' inside of me. I attacked him
Faye. I fuckin'—I—I attacked him. I attacked my supervisor. I'm—- I'm done. I just . . . I went for him. Just for a
second. Like a shockwave went through me. Lunged at
him like I was gonna pound him into the fuckin' ground.
Like I was gonna grab him by the collar and crush that
shit in my hands. Looked at him in his eyes. Seein'
through that emptiness. That lack of feeling. That—whatever you call it—that make you stop seein' yourself in
somebody else. And I flexed on him like- "Nigga I wish
you would say some shit like that again. I will fuckin'
kill you." 'Cept I ain't say it with words. *(beat)* Then
the shockwave left me. Real fast. And I ain't touch him
at all. Just got swole on ‹him for a sec. But I came close
enough. I would've. And he know it. And I know it too.
I see him looking into my eyes like I'm the devil. Can
smell his fear. Like if he even breathes louder than a
sigh I might kill him dead. And I might've Faye. I just
might've. *(beat)* And I stand there, froze. Not knowin'
if I really reached at him or if it was in my mind. But I

see him lookin' at me-stiff. Like I scared the shit outta him. Like he was under attack. Like I'm that nigga. It's nothin' but silence between us for a sec. And then I just say, "NO DEAL." And I walk out.

Dramatic

Peter Lorre, thirty-eight

Peter Lorre is speaking to his friend Humphrey Bogart. Lorre has stolen John Barrymore's dead body from the mortuary and wants to put it in Jack Warner's house to protest the studio system. He needs Bogart's help, but Bogart keeps stalling.

LORRE: Not another wasted night drinking booze and chasing girlies! That is what *you* want! You are content to be the last loser left in Hollywoodland making B-pictures, and worshipping your idol, your Errol Flynn. Do you know he's got syphilis, do you know he's got a constant case of clap and worse, do you know he still diddles fourteen year old girls, of course you know. And I hear he's got TB to boot. Some idol. And he's a foreigner too! Just the right kind I guess. *(beat)* Don›t get me wrong, God bless your troops, your forty thousand dead, but look at you, *you* American, secluded in the hills, caught in a cycle of perpetual masturbation, from nowhere, nowhere bound! How could *you* understand *me*? I believe in the power of the theater! I played parts in poverty, begging for bread, sleeping on benches, taking morphine only because my appendix threatened my theatrical career. As an actor, I can change people, by making them relate to a person they didn't know they could relate to, by helping them see life from another perspective, by helping them see themselves from another perspective, by increasing their empathy and thus decreasing their hatred! Acting is making Nazis cry over the death of a Jew. That is what I am capable of! But you, for you acting is serving an audience a sadistic thrill, force feeding them American dream lies by manipulating them with disjointed pictures. There is no empathy, there is only fantasy. People they'll never be as good-looking as, as brave as, as tough as, dames they'll never get, money they'll never make. Heroics they'll always fall short of. You wake up every morning and sell your piss to the urinal! In this marketplace of lies! You make laxatives for the soul! It is scarcely possible for me to stand in the same room as you, *you* drug pusher, *you* spiritual cripple, *you* moral invalid!

For information on this author, click on the WRITERS tab at www.smithandkraus.com.

Dramatic
Will, twenty-eight, Chinese-American

Will, a programmer with a new idea for an ed tech startup, tries to persuade a close friend from college with a cushy trust fund to be his first investor.

WILL: *Classrooms are broken.* Imagine if you went into a hospital with appendicitis and the doctor pulled out a bottle of ether and a hack saw. There is no other industry where it's still considered okay to do things the way they were done in the nineteenth century. But in schools . . . It's still one grownup, standing at the front of the class, talking to a huge bunch of kids. Like it's 1800. Like it's Ancient Greece. I want to change that. I want to be able to say that was me, I changed that. Not just I made 5% off of a good pick, but I made something. This is a growth field. This is the moment to go into it. Edtech is the new frontier, it's the new social networking, I think in a couple years, everyone is going to be going into it. Not doing it now will be like - saying no to Facebook five years ago. You'd want to fucking shoot yourself. You'd never get over the fact that you didn't do it. And the best thing is - it's good for everyone. Students learn more, teachers have more time, we make money. Everybody wins. Think about it - education. It fixes everything. If you have better education, you have people being smart enough to look at advertising and mortgages and news coverage with some basic critical thinking skills. Think about kids across America being smarter because of you, and the economy running better because of you, and voters voting more intelligently because of you. Like your grandfather, right? I mean every time you see made in Taiwan stuck on something, that was him.

He changed everything. I'm going to change everything. And all I need is a little bit of money.

Dramatic
Finn, thirties

*Finn works as a line cook at a dive bar in Massachu-
setts. Here, he tells a secret about himself to Jimmy,
the karaoke host, after he confesses to not helping a
long-time friend end his life.*

FINN: Think about if that was you. You know, think about,
like, you had a daughter, granddaughter, whatever - but
the person who means the most to you, right? And you
know, in your gut, that pretty soon you're gonna be a
fuckin' anvil tied to her ankle. What would you want?
God, I . . . this whole time D's been back, I thought she
was here because that was the only real choice there
was. Come to find out, all that time before she gave up
everything, this bullshit happened? What is that? Man,
why the fuck you had to tell me that? You know . . . shit.
Shit, mother fucker . . . Dude, I can't do anything for her!
You know who I am? I'm . . . fuck it. FUCK. IT. I'm a
pansy ass, broke his own wrist to get himself outta the
Marines. Put it right between the bars of a water heater,
snapped the fucker clean in half. POP! Just like that.
That's fucked up, but it worked. Dishonorable discharge.
Never went back, never looked back, never grew up,
never went anywhere, never did a thing but hide in the
back of some bar, restaurant, food truck, behind a grill.
Fuckin' have to spatula everything southpaw, cause this
shit's all but useless *(indicating his right wrist)*. I'm like
36 goin' on 16! I got no money, I live in a basement with
leaky pipes, no woman worth having would ever sign her
name to that - not D, not anybody! That's what my life
is. But you know, but I can still - I can somehow show
up and I do what I gotta do, and at the very least, try to
be a guy that's there if someone needs someone, even if

it's just a minute - like a mere 60 seconds. If I can be a guy that helps just that much, maybe, just maybe, even if I have monumentally fucked up my whole life, I might still mean something in this world. So you know, so fuck you, dude. Because I tell you what, I would'a done it. Ernie asked me to leave him a gun, I would'a done it. And I would'a done it for you, or my own grandfather, or my father, or anybody. You know why? Because it ain't worth living, to feel like you're a burden to the only person who matters to you. And when you're done with this life, you should respectfully be able to bow the fuck out, no questions asked.

For information on this author, click on the WRITERS tab at www.smithandkraus.com.

Dramatic
Finn, thirties

Finn is a line cook at a local dive bar. After a cancelled memorial service for a local business owner and friend, he confesses to his estranged love, Deirdre, how he really feels about her, and the town they live in.

FINN: The sex sort of isn't the point. Well, it's some of the point, but the real point is, us together, tangled up, half dressed. Afterwards. You looked at me all pink and . . . beautiful. Swore you were gonna say . . . (I love you), but you didn't. Instead you said, "Puppy, what's the thing you're most afraid of?" Maybe you don't remember, but I do. This was my answer. Tonight was my answer. I told you, I was most afraid, that one day, when I died, that nobody would show up to my funeral. That I didn't mean enough to anyone, so when I died, all there'd be left of my life would be booze and a shallow grave, and nobody to care I was gone. I mean, it didn't exactly go down like that for Ernie, but close enough. And I'm not even a tenth of the man he was. And I think . . . I think that tells you . . . shit, you're right, baby. We're livin' in a graveyard of what life used to be. And this is the end of the world. Home or not, we stay here, we die here, we just saw what that day is gonna look like. So what I'm trying to . . . my whole life, I hid behind something, or someone. Never believed I'd be much. And maybe that's true. But maybe, it's only cause I've made it true. I mean, if I can teach myself Elvish . . . I'm saying that . . . last night, what that was, felt right to me. And I think it did to you too. I'm saying that no matter what, some things don't change. Some things never change. Twenty years ago, twenty years from now, sometimes, once you have something, you always have it. Like the fact that I fuckin' love you.

For information on this author, click on the WRITERS tab at www.smithandkraus.com.

Dramatic
Steven, late thirties - early forties

Steven is at a table at a restaurant, shared by his husband, Stephen, and their best friend, Carrie. The group; has met to celebrate Steven's birthday, but there is something that has upset him. Here, he tells their waiter, Estaban, what has gotten him so bent out of shape.

STEVEN: ONCE UPON A TIME . . . or more specifically: once upon sometime this morning, Crown Prince Zack, our 8 year old son, "borrowed" the latest generation iPhone of my partner Stephen. Zack "borrows" things. We have no idea why. We hope it's a phase. "What's the matter with kids today", huh? Anyway, this afternoon, in the course of my lonely parental duties extracting said iPhone from Zachary's sticky-fingered clutches —sticky-fingered both metaphorically and literally because god knows what he was eating—I was greeted with a series of little surprises, little nuggets, that "twinkled and shim-mered and buzzed" at regular intervals over the adorable screenshot of our son and his cat, Elphaba. These virtual haiku. These cyber tone poems? They were chock full —no cock-full—of rather ambitious assignments for Ste-phen, my partner of 16 years, to perform upon or with or into (or whatever) the ass / mouth / dick / ears nose throat / oh and this was a surprise, FEET—of Brian, the Significant God-Knows-What of my oldest friend in the world Matt. Hey Matt! SURPRISE, right?! It's always been our dream for Brian and Stephen to get along better and look: NOW THEY DO! So, Esteban, what happened was that after an agonizing afternoon of excru-ciating indecision—I came tonight, to this, my birthday party, determined to, I don't know what. But I came. Determined. Because I like a good party, and because Matt and Carrie and I, we always do our birthdays, and then, let's see, I ordered a Vodka Stinger and would like another when you have a chance please, and then after enduring some vaguely-amusing pleasantries and a spirited round of "Ooo What a Hot Foreign Waiter!" (and own it, Esteban, because it fades), for reasons that I hope are now clear, things starting spinning a little out of control and so what happened was that I could not stand this bullshit for even one more millisecond and that your well-appointed table became collateral damage IN STEPHEN'S COMPLETE AND TOTAL ANNIHILATION OF WHAT WAS ONCE BUT WILL NEVER BE AGAIN OUR PICTURE-PERFECT STORYBOOK FAIRY TALE EXISTENCE.

For information on this author, click on the WRITERS tab at www.smithandkraus.com.

Seriocomic
Steven, late thirties-early forties

Steve and his husband Stephen have separated after Steven found that Stephen was sexting another man. In retaliation, he had sex with Estaban, a waiter/dancer. Here, he laments the whole mess to his friend, Carrie.

STEVEN: Why isn't Stephen here? Why hasn't he come crawling back? And why did I make him request all those songs when I loved him right from "Some Enchanted Evening?" How could I have been so cruel? And where is my son? Why isn't he here? And why does he steal? And why does he scream in his sleep? And why in the world did he pick *the trombone*? And why did I sleep with Esteban? And why did I sleep with Esteban again — and why did I sleep with Esteban again after that? And how does he manage to hold down a hundred thousand jobs *and volunteer*? Why isn't being a mother everything I thought it would be? And how am I going to find a job? Doing what? What in the world am I qualified to do? And why did my father leave? Was it because I cried when he gave me the fishing rod? Or did I scare him off with my one boy version of the Pacific Overtures cast album? And why, God help me, do I like Stephen's mom *so* much better than mine? And why have I found Brian so unbelievably attractive from the moment I met him? *Why didn't he sext me?* And why am I still miffed that Tammy Grimes—and it was Tammy Grimes, my love, vomiting all over the restaurant that magical night, not Jean Simmons not Glynnis Johns—why did Tammy Grimes only want to sing with you? And how can I hate you, because *I do*, for getting sick? And then for moving in? And now for . . . leaving? Could I be a bigger asshole? 11-11-15 And why do I hate Stephen *so much*? All he's done is give me everything I've ever him asked for. And love me . . . I guess . . . in his way. *Why am I so angry? AND WHAT KIND OF GOD WOULD ALLOW THE MOVIE VERSION OF MAME?*!! Why am I going on like this? What's my problem? What do I do?

For information on this author, click on the WRITERS tab at www.smithandkraus.com.

Dramatic
Paul, thirties

Paul is speaking to his wife, Donna, as they sit in the backyard of their home at 2am, waiting for their fifteen year old son to come home so that they can take him to drug rehab. Soon they begin to question everything in their home, including their possible complicity in their son's addiction.

PAUL: Think about it. My father was an alcoholic. Your brother is manic depressive . . . our genes mixed up this insane cocktail that makes our son compelled to do drugs. That's on us. And, what's worse, we set all this in motion and now we can't even stop him because of our own limitations. We can't even talk to our own child like he's our child because we don't even know him. He might as well be someone else's kid. Just because we made him, doesn't mean we know him. It's arrogant to think that. That's such an arrogant thought. I see this all so clearly now. Our gene pool mapped out this little trap for him to walk into and we're so broken now because of it . . . we're so tainted in our own thinking processes . . . our own presumptions about who he is and what he needs . . . .just overflowing with NA and AA and Al-Anon and every other "go-fuck-yourself-on paper bullshit dogma" that we have forgotten how to talk to our kid like he was our child and not a problem we have to fix. Not a bathroom to paint. A yard to "re-imagine." We're so broken and damaged that we think our drug ad- dicted son is an appliance. We think he comes with blue-prints. We're going to pay some rehab facility to take him away from us and just handle it. Our son is dry cleaning. Our son is the car in the shop. And even if we do get him off drugs, he's still gone.

Dramatic
Paul, thirties

*It's 2am and, who has been waiting in his backyard
for his fifteen-year-old son to come home so that he
can take him to drug rehab, is arguing with his can-
tankerous next door neighbor, Mrs. Johnston, who
has just woken up because of Paul's yelling. When
Mrs. Johnston nastily suggests that their son is in
the predicament that he is in because of Paul's poor
parenting skills, Paul angrily erupts.*

PAUL: You hear that? We don't want to be on your stupid,
ass sucking, planning committee anyway. And hey — go
right ahead, call the police. I'm begging you to call the
police because then I can tell them how you still receive
social security checks from dead Mr. Johnston. Yeah,
didn't think I knew about that huh? That's right. DON-
NA She really does that? Paul nods. PAUL Oh and Mrs.
Johnston? Just so we're clear. I think St. Rocco is the
most unnecessary Saint ever invented in the history of
the Catholic Church!! That's right! (MORE) 68. How do
you like that? How does that work for you? He's totally
extraneous and, I suspect . . . a little bit Guido. That's
right, Mrs. Johnston . . . he's got a little New Jersey
in him! Which reminds me, speaking of the Garden State,
the Church has so many Saints, it's a shame there's no
Saint for yard maintenance because we'd be praying to
that Saint right now—on our hands and knees at the forest
of plant and scum that is your backyard, Mrs. Johnston.
Oh, wait a minute, I forgot. We can't do that. We can't
get on our hands and knees to pray to that hypothetical
Catholic Saint. Do you know why, Mrs. Johnston? Because we're not Catholic! That's right, we lied during our

interview just to get on the planning committee! Nope. There's not a confessional booth between us! We're Episcopalian! Yeah, that's right, Mrs. Johnston. Episcopalian —the other white Christians! We're the ones without all the lawsuits. So why don't you go back in your house and pray to all your needless saints, and continue to defraud the American government while we get on, waiting for our son, in the land of the living and legal! Run a long now, Mrs. Johnston!

Dramatic
Nick, thirty-five

Nick speaks to his daughter Teenie for the first time since injuring her as an infant.

NICK: Ya know, when you were newborn . . . my God, I never knew a kid with so much personality. That face . . . you were so alive and . . . I would talk to you just like I am now, no bullshit, no baby-talk, just real conversation, ya know and . . . you spoke right back as best you knew how to, and let me tell you, it made more damn sense than half the stuff people say to me. I told you things I'll never tell anyone, stuff I couldn't go to your mother with, I came to you . . . the only person ever to really listen. Sometimes I would even ask your advice on certain matters, I mean real life questions, and just watch you try to answer. I don't know what the hell advice I ever expected out of a three month old, I just loved seein you try to answer me, you wanted to *so* bad *(beat)* . . . so bad, you even seemed upset when it was only noise comin out, but for *me* . . . that's all I needed to hear for whatever was eatin me to seem a little less important. There were real thoughts goin through that little head, you just didn't know how to say em yet, and I could see how much of a bother that was. *(Beat)* Looks like it still bothers you a little bit. *(Smiles)* "Other babies are just babies, poor things, but *this* kid . . . " *(Starts to laugh a bit)* guys at work got pissed after a while, that's all they ever heard, like their own kids didn't matter, but hey, what could I say, you were somethin else . . . that urge to communicate right off the bat, I never saw it in someone so small, you *could not wait* to start talkin. *(Laughter dies)* I'm awful sorry that never ended up happenin for you, I could tell how much you were lookin forward to it. *(Withholding)* Shit, I was lookin forward to finally hearin all the things you had to say . . . and ya know what, I think we might'a had some good talks, the two of us. And I'm sure you'da been smarter than me by now, that much I know *(sad laughter which dies right away)* . . . be getting ready to leave for college, ready to be whatever it was you were meant to be . . . startin to turn into that anyway. Instead, here you are, still waitin on that first word. *(Smiling on a humorous memory)* You . . . your mother went nuts with all the noise you made, you almost even made her cry one time, it was all I could do not to laugh out loud *(laughs a bit)* . . . see it never bothered me as much cuz I knew what all the noise was about . . . and anytime I saw you were gettin upset, I always made this promise, I said "listen kiddo . . . you'll be talkin my ear off soon enough, I promise you that, so don'chu worry about it, just hang in there and be patient, it'll happen." *(Beat)* I wasn't lyin about that, ya know, I want you to know I wasn't tellin a lie. I never meant to shut you up for good, it was just that *one time*, I *(beat)* . . . I don't know why babies have to be so breakable. I just hate to think you still been waitin on that promise all this time. *(Examines her face closely)* Looks to me though like maybe you *(stunning realization)* . . . you *still* wanna speak, even now, don'chu? *(Looks even closer)* Yep, I didn't notice at first but I recognize those eyes now, you still got that same look, like you been waitin all along to say what'chu gotta say. Maybe I'm delusional, I don't know, but that's what it seems like to me, and I'm your father, so . . . whatever it is, you can say it to me right now, I know you can't make the words and I'm sorry for that, but . . . well I was always able to understand you anyway, ya know? Whatever you wanna say, you know I'll get it . . . we have an understanding, you'n me . . .

For information on this author, click on the WRITERS tab at www.smithandkraus.com.

Seriocomic
Jack, late thirties-early forties

Jack has just found out that he has a lump, which is probably cancer. His neighbor, Bill, was supposed to pick him up at the hospital but he forgot so he called his ex, Diane, who arrived at the hospital with her new boyfriend, Ralph (she calls him "Rafe"), in his new truck. Diane has told Jack that she and Ralph are moving to Texas and taking Jack's kids with them. Here Jack tells his neighbor Bill what happened when he persuaded Ralph to let him drive Ralph's new truck.

JACK: I decide against wrecking the truck, but then I think how could I give it a good ding? Just enough to sabotage Ralph's new car glow, tie him up with insurance paperwork for weeks. Simultaneously, I'm processing Diane's big news, I'm driving like a crazy man, she tells me to slow down, she's sounding like a wife again, and I'm *enjoying* it only then she has to open her yap one more time, "Be careful. Rafe's in the back" and I realize, her concern is not for *me*, for *us*, not even for the *truck*, but for *Rafe* so when we get to my street, this street, I cut the corner like a son of a bitch, I cut it like a rodeo horse, and at that moment, praise Allah, our friend Ralph who's been sitting on top of the built-in and, I predict, completely empty tool chest, realizes he's been sitting in a puddle. He stands up to brush off his Dockers, he lets go, and all of a sudden he's airborne, he goes flying out of the truck. He lands, and this is the beauty part, he lands on top of *my* car which is parked at the curb . . . And he's so *fat* he breaks the sunroof. There's a crack the length of the Continental Divide! He's climbing down from the roof, brushing himself off, pulling the wet khaki away from his fat ass, trying to regain his dignity, trying to look like he *meant* to do that, trying not to look the putz he is in front of Diane. And he says, real cool, "So Jack how'd you like the new truck?" And I say, "It's a little loose on the turns." Diane's freaking out! "Call 911! Call 911!" Totally overreacting. The man's got enough fat on him to cushion a fall from the top of the Empire State Building. And he's going "I'm alright baby, I'm alright, baby." *Baby*. It's like one of those soap opera words. It makes my skin crawl. She's like "We do you a favor and blah blah blah." And I'm like, "A favor, a *favor*, I give you twenty years of my life and when I'm dying from a cancer you can't give me a ride home from the hospital?!" and she's like "You didn't give me squat" (*Rafe's voice*) "There, there baby" "You didn't give me *squat*!" He's trying to calm her down, cause she's all alley cat now, she's coming at me all elbows and fingernails, and when Ralph comes between us she pushes him the hell outta the way, causing him to fall against the truck! He grabs for something to hold on to, finds the side view mirror, pulls on it with all his weight so he won't hit the ground and accidentally snaps it off! His big he-man truck has Made in China written all over it! And now he's like totally forgotten about Diane, he's like *obsessing* about the warranty, searching through the glove compartment with his ass sticking out the passenger door like the moon rising over Alabama and she's looking at him like "Who is this asshole?"

For information on this author, click on the WRITERS tab at www.smithandkraus.com.

Seriocomic
Jack, late thirties-early forties

*This is a continuation of the previous monologue.
On the way home from the hospital, Jack resisted the
temptation to wreck Ralph's truck but when he took
a corner too fast, Ralph went flying out of the back.
Furious, his ex-wife Diane reminds Jack of how he
used to lie about going to AA meetings when he was
actually with his mistress. Here, Jack tells Bill what
happened next.*

JACK: Diane goes, "You are so *not* dying of cancer! You
have a *lump*! People have lumps all the time! *I* had a
lump! *Rafe* had a lump!" Suddenly everybody's got a
lump. And I'm like, "You think I'm making this *up*?"
And she says, "It wouldn't be the first time. Remember
the AA meetings Jack? Remember that?" They're like
elephants. They never forget. So he's like "Baby, get in
the truck, baby, get in the truck!" And she goes, "Don't
call me baby!" She was my hero! But he wants a piece
of me now, so he throws a punch, it's a total whiff, an
air ball, but it's enough to get her on my side, and now
she's screaming, "What the hell are you doing? The man's
got *cancer*!" So I egg him on. "Go ahead, kick my ass!"
I say, "I'm on painkiller anyway!" By now, Diane's in
the truck, key in the ignition, barking out orders like Lou
Gosset, Jr. "Ralph!" She forgets to call him Rafe. "Ralph,
get in the fucking truck!" I can see this guy's pea brain
short-circuiting. What is the manly thing to do? Pummel
a man with cancer! Or run to Mama? She goes, "Get
into this truck or I swear to God, I'll run you both over
and leave you for dead! Birds of prey will peck out your
eyes!" Where this guy comes from women don't talk that

way, I can see his thoughts like a little cartoon thought bubble, "I'm going to Texas with a crazy woman," but he's scared enough to get in the truck, on the passenger side, which makes him look totally dick-less. But before they pull out, he rolls down the window, actually he buttons down the made-in-China power window, which gets stuck so he has to sort of rest his chin on the glass like a Labrador Retriever, and he says, "You'll be hearing from my lawyer." And I'm like, "Guess what? I *know* lawyers. I *work* with lawyers. I am friends with the entire American Bar Association! And not one of them is going to give a fuck about a side-view mirror on a toy truck!" It doesn't matter what the courts say. Fat Ralph is taking my children to Texas and if I ever see them again, they'll be pulling those little rolling suitcases that all the small, sad divorced kids drag through airports. *(beat)* So, that was my day. How was *your* day?

For information on this author, click on the WRITERS tab at www.smithandkraus.com.

Seriocomic
Lance, early twenties

Lance is going over a declaration of love he has written.

LANCE: This Is a Test . . . but not of the Emergency Broadcasting System. My entire life I've been a perpetual student. Some people might say a virtual student, but it's real.

(looking at notebook trying to memorize)

I need you, honey. Ever since I met you . . .

(Looks up.)

. . . my life has . . .

(Looks down again at notebook and then looks up.)

. . . been on fire. You have capitulated . . .

(Looks down questionably, then looks back up.)

. . . captivated me

(Crosses out on notebook and writes revised word.)

And you have influenced me in every decision I have to make forever. I'll offer you gainful employment. I had three interviews last week for internships. I know you work for nothing but it leads to a big job. You see, I can play the game. Number 2 . . .

(Looks down at notes again and then looks up.)

. . . Companionship. We can travel the world together. Only the two of us. No one else counts. As long as we're together everyone else is

(Looks down and reads)

. . . nonessential.

(Looks up again.)

We are each other's soulmates. And number 3. I'll be your . . . lover. I know this is an important pre-requisite. I know you want to prove first that we are compatible. That's another thing that I love about you. You're so practical. Oh, I love you, I love you, I love you. Was that satisfactory, *mon Cherie*? Did it send off all the correct bells and whistles. Tick all the right boxes. That is just a small sampling of what you'll get every night in our future together, my dear. So I have crammed for this test like I have no other. Now what is it again? How can I forget? No. 1 is . . . It doesn't really matter the order of things now does it? Just that you need a job. You need a place to live. A high speed online connection. And you need love and companionship and sex. So what about it? Is our life over or just beginning?

For information on this author, click on the WRITERS tab at www.smithandkraus.com.

Seriocomic
Doug, twenties

*Doug has come to a couple's apartment for a sexual
threesome, but has just had diarrhea. He has cleaned
himself up, and tells them a story about the last time
this happened to him.*

DOUG: Geez, second time you'd think I'd learn. It should
really teach me not to eat before sex. Protein's fine to get
your stamina up but lay off the curries. Oddly enough
the last time this happened to me started the same place I
met you; at the publishing house. It was a party to launch
some book. Funny story this, I have to tell you. So I'm at
this party. And I see this smart, really attractive woman.
This was a year before I met you just so you don't think
I'm some man-whore or anything. Anyway. And I won't
tell you who this woman was except to say she was the
last publisher's daughter. So that didn't hurt. I hadn't yet
gotten on their radar as a photographer slash book de-
signer. Anyway: one thing leads to another and we end up
back at her place. And, you know, we're kissing; taking
off our clothes. All kinds of juices are flowing. But I'm
also beginning to feel my stomach rumble. Because at
the launch party the caterer had been serving Thai food,
which I love. Chicken Satay with spicy peanut sauce. Pad
Thai with prawns. Lamb cutlets. Squid *and* desserts. I'm
a starving artist, so I'm shoveling it in. And the food is
on - it starts to go on spin cycle at some point, with all
the stomach acid. And I'm feeling that tug to take a crap,
you know? When your lower stomach is feeling like a
crapped-in diaper. God, I can't believe I'm telling you
this. But: but: there's no way I can excuse myself. You
can't excuse yourself to take a crap on a first date. Maybe

on a fifth or sixth. With us it's different. But anyway, I'm thinking, I can hold it in. I can pucker up that muscle until it's over. But here's the thing. I discover she's really into teasing a guy *in that area*. You know? Which normally I would find exciting. That's an under-utilized erogenous zone in my book, and we can definitely explore it if you want. But at the time I had to slap her hand away, because I was trying to keep a tight lid on things. But the more I slap her hand away, the more she thinks it's a game. And this is the kind of girl who's used to getting her way, you know, with the privileged upbringing she's had. And just when I think we've moved on to other things and my guard is down, she wets that finger of hers and pops that sucker in. *Boom.* My sphincter muscle instantly dilates like it's taking a big yawn and out comes all of that Thai food in an instant rush of liquid crap. *Whoosh.* I could not hold it in. All over her thousand thread count sheet or whatever it was. And she was *not* understanding. Which I got: who wants to bring home a date who craps all over your expensive sheets? She could not move past it. That was like a red line for her . . . There was another point to this story . . .

(Tries to recall but can't.)

Anyway . . . I hope I wasn't sharing too much.

Dramatic
Rashid, twenties

*Rashid is having second thoughts about agreeing to
participate in a threesome, as he tells Leila when the
guy they have invited over leaves the room.*

RASHID: I have to confess . . . I'm . . . I'm not warming up
to him . . . .I'm not even sure I . . . particularly like him
. . . . I was on the fence before, now . . . now I'm not. I
don't want someone else touching you . . . . I thought I
could do this in some . . . theoretical place where fantasies like this play out. But in the flesh?—No. I can't.
Thought I could. Can't. Call me possessive. I must be
weird that way. I don't know what we were thinking.
—It's like we have to . . . or I have to constantly prove
something to you. And I don't know what it is I'm trying
to prove. That I . . . ? That I'm not like other guys? That
I understand and respect your freedoms? That I believe
in your right to have your fantasies? What? Everything
feels like such a battle with you; and I don't know what
the battle's about anymore. *(Small pause.)* Leila:—do
you need this guy to make you feel attractive?—Is that
it?—Is there a particular way he looks at you that I›m
not . . . .That makes you feel something that you don›t
feel with me anymore?

THE TRIUMPHANT RETURN OF BLACKBIRD FLYNT

Peter Ullian

Dramatic
Morgan, forties

*Morgan was a disillusioned casualty of the sixties,
until he met self-proclaimed revolutionary Blackbird
Flynt and joined up with his band of misfits, an amal-
gam of old radicals and young punks dedicated to
overthrowing the government in mid-1980s America.
After a failed bank robbery, however, some if the band
are having doubts. Morgan, still holding on to the
dream, tries to remind his comrades why Blackbird
is their leader.*

MORGAN: You remember the time you got thrown in jail,
Thompson? When they caught you packing heat, even
if it was only a starter's pistol? Remember that? Who
got you out? Blackbird Flynt. He walked right in there
in a three-piece suit and pretended to be your lawyer.
Remember that? And he scared the shit out of those cops.
They thought they were gonna get their butts sued. He
had them thinking that they'd violated every Goddamn
constitutional article in the Bill of Rights, and a few that
hadn't even been adopted yet. And you were out walking
around in an hour's time. Remember that? Blackbird's
given us . . . a reason. I mean . . . at one time, I used
to think at one time that there was nothing worth doing anymore. Everything had been done. And it hadn't
worked. I used to think that there was nothing left in life
but pure, hedonistic pleasure. Art, books, philosophy,
religion . . . they were all an old ticket to me. So, after I
was other-than-honorably-discharged, I rode around in a
Ford convertible and drank. Drank Jack Daniels. Fucked
around. A lot. But then one day I took a swig of J.D.
and it tasted different. Didn't go down as smooth.

I'm looking around at what I'm doing, it's O.K., it's fun, I'm spending a lot of energy, I'm driving fast, I'm getting drunk, I'm feeling good. But I'm bored. Because there's nothing else for me to do. And that didn't seem right. In fact, that seemed wrong. If all the world's got to offer me is whiskey and cars, which are great, I mean I like whiskey and cars, they're fine — but if that's all there is . . . then something is definitely wrong. And I thought, maybe if I took all this energy and redirected it, maybe I could try to rearrange the world, instead of just rearranging my brain cells. Well, I wasn't going to run for office. So I decided to subvert. I decided to attack. Whatever I could find to attack. I decided that was the only road to progress. Attack. Take the other route. Take the underground route. So I began to harass the local police station with crank phone calls. Ordered pizza and shit like that. Well, they got used to me, they hung up. I was young, Thompson, younger than even you, and almost as dumb. Well, maybe not that dumb. The point is, before you attack you've got to have something more, you've got to have a target, you've got to have a plan, you've got to have a vision, you've got to have a reason for your revolution. I didn't have those things. I needed to find someone who did. I didn't have anybody. I was lonely. A lonely revolutionary. So, I went to the movies. Looking for somebody. Somebody to inspire me. And I found myself identifying, not with the hero, not with the anti-hero, not even with the number one bad-guy, but with the cheap, slimy hood who does all the dirty work and gets killed about a half an hour before the end of the film. I saw myself as Vic Morrow. It wasn't that I wanted to get killed, it was just that I saw myself in that function, but not working for Sydney Greenstreet or anybody like that, but working for the hero. The man with the vision. The hero and his henchman. The hero never had a henchman. He had a sidekick, but never a henchman. The hero never had a cheap, slimy hood to do all his dirty work. And I just couldn't get it out of my head how much better off we'd all be if he did. *(Beat.)* You always wanted to be the hero, didn›t you, Blackbird?

For information on this author, click on the WRITERS tab at www.smithandkraus.com.

Dramatic
Bruno, 22

*Bruno sits in the freezing cold with his father, who
has frozen to death, sharing his fears of ending up
like him.*

BRUNO: You're not going back there, Dad, the place is shut down. Nobody's in there anymore, that's why you're out here freezing to death . . . and I was only trying to bring you home . . . I'm not leaving here without you, so we can sit here all night but we are leaving here together . There you go . . . that's better now . . . first time you stopped shivering since I got here. Sorry I never came to see you . . . I just don't like that place . . . no less than you, though, I'm sure . . . and I can't blame you for not knowin me, I should'a come to visit. *(beat)* You know, it was hard enough growing up *knowing* my parents were crazy . . . but that was before I started thinkin you might not be . . . You remember when Mom would lock me out because I was a robot who killed me and put on my skin? Well it wasn't easy bein locked out on nights as cold as this one…but at least I could brush it all off with the snow on my shoulders . . . 'at was until one day I decided to take a knife down to my bone just to make sure I wasn't wires and circuits. *(Beat)* I don't…know what's real and what's not real . . . I . . . I just can't tell anymore . . . day to day I walk through this dream . . . not a nightmare . . . just a really strange dream that leaves me completely restless. I'll never forget the day when something she said . . . *actually* made sense to me . . . like I finally understood her . . . logic . . . what I thought was nonsense before started to seem . . . somewhat plausible . . . and the older I get the better I understand her and I can't help but think that means . . . ya know . . . today was the worst of it, I felt like it was a turning point, I wished it wasn't, but I don't know anymore . . . I don't wanna be like the two'a'you . . . I'm *scared* . . . I mean look at you! I just wanna live a normal life with a normal family . . . but I mean suppose there's nuthin wrong with either one'a'you . . . suppose there'somethin wrong with everyone else just like she said? Like we're in on somethin no one else can understand . . . and enlightenment only seems like insanity . . . maybe you'n Ma had it all figured out from the start . . . and I'm ju'starting to understand it all . . . Maybe I'm crazy but...I'd like to think that we're special. I mean maybe we really are, you know? (*Beat*) Nobody sees what we see because *we . . . are* special . . . like no one else in the world.

For information on this author, click on the WRITERS tab at www.smithandkraus.com.

Seriocomic
The Guy with Nothing, ageless

THE GUY WITH NOTHING is a thanatological angel. He is the play's narrator, the Greek chorus. He introduces us to all the other characters, and comments casually and deeply on the action. He speaks to the audience, and can be any age at all. He is blue-collar, casual and conversational. He is both of this world and another; he is matter-of-fact and genuine. The rules of his existence are fungible. Sometimes and to some people he is visible; in other situations and to other people, he is not. No sense can or needs be made of this.

THE GUY WITH NOTHING: No one smokes anymore, people give you a dirty look. I think it's a shame, about the smoking. Smoking is terrific. Just because something has catastrophic consequences doesn't mean it's not terrific. Smoking feels wonderful. You know. You have this whole body, these whole insides and no one sees it or admits it. When someone's lying dead with their brains or guts or whatever sticking out, we get all horrified, but it's actually a kind of excitement we never get. It's arousing! That's why there's all that murder in the movies! You never get to see those things that we're fucking made of! When do you see it? I mean, there are these assholes who faint at the sight of blood! The thing about smoking: You actually feel the shape of your lungs. The lungs are terrific! They run long and deep, from the top of the chest all the way down to your belt buckle, you can picture them in your mind in great detail when you inhale a cigarette. You can actually be closer to an idea that you are made of lungs when you insult them with a cigarette.

This insult describes them clearly in your mind. There's something distancing about showing great respect. It's like a mountain or something. High and far away. With an insult comes closeness. You see what I'm getting at? I love smoking. They're looking at me all nasty outside, I'm puffing away under the awning, it's raining, I'm trying to keep my cigarette dry. But they looked at me! These are people who wouldn't even have looked at me to insult me with their eyes if I weren't smoking! I wanted to kiss them! I wanted to kiss each one of them!

For information on this author, click on the WRITERS tab at www.smithandkraus.com.

Dramatic
The Guy with Nothing. Ageless

THE GUY WITH NOTHING is a thanatological angel. He is the play's narrator, the Greek chorus. He introduces us to all the other characters, and comments casually and deeply on the action. He speaks to the audience, and can be any age at all. He is blue-collar, casual and conversational. He is both of this world and another; he is matter-of-fact and genuine. The rules of his existence are fungible. Sometimes and to some people he is visible; in other situations and to other people, he is not. No sense can or needs be made of this.

THE GUY WITH NOTHING: I haven't been completely straight with you, anyway. I haven't told you the whole story. But that's okay. It doesn't make me a liar, it's not like you asked me a lot of stuff and I pretended to give you the complete answer and left out everything that mattered. Anyway, the thing I'm thinking about is, I spend most of my time sitting on the old woman's shoulder. It's a narrow shoulder, not much to cry on. But I sit there. When I sit there, I'm not visible. I'm the one who will collect her. I'm the one. That's my duty. I spend quite a lot of time with those two. I like them quite alright, really, even though they should be in a novel, not a play. The woman I sit on, she ignores me, my weight, the trouble I cause her. She ignores her own infirmity, her own claustrophobia and inconvenience. But the man. He looks for me all the time. He doesn't see me, but he always thinks he does. Does this sound confusing? It's actually funny, once you see it clearly. I sit on her shoulder, waiting for just the right moment to disappear with her, and days go by. See. Days go by. I've taken to looking out one of her windows, the one she faces when she's watching the cooking shows and the lady Judge who yells at everybody what an idiot they are. I can't really see those shows, same as she can't really see ME. So I look out the window: that I can see. There's a man, lives in the house next door, he lives alone, his wife and children left him. I saw the wife once, briefly. Something was wrong with her, there was this terrible anger she had going. She looked okay, except some dirty part of her mind made her look bruised and ugly. She yelled like wind. Then she left with the children; skinny, mangy little things. The man next door, I look at him all the time, through the window. He doesn't go out. He smokes. There's a big dog he has, that howls. He ties it up outside, and it suffers for him, it howls. It's not my fault this is a play, so don't blame me. Anyways. I should tell you, this man is naked most of the time. It's like he's trying to forgive himself his body. It's like a confrontation between two angry people, him and his body. He walks around, smoking, he strikes himself on the chest, the shoulder, the thigh. He paces. The dog howls, and he paces. I love looking at this naked man. I don't have a chance to see this simple thing, this simple organization of limb and muscle, you know, this arrangement of tissue that is the body of someone. I love looking at him. I stare at him for hours, while the old woman stares at the Judge, the old man stares for me, and I sit on the shoulder, watching a man howl without howling, fighting with his body.

For information on this author, click on the WRITERS tab at www.smithandkraus.com.

Joshua James

Dramatic
Maynard, twenty-nine

Maynard, a suicidal poet, is speaking to Roscoe, a department store dummy in his apartment as he watches Ginny, the girl he invited in, sleep.

MAYNARD: She does have a pretty face, though, doesn't she, Roscoe? Faces. Fucking faces. Can't trust 'em. I remember the first face I ever really looked into, other than my parents. The first time I ever saw someone else's, that's when I knew all was not right in the really-real world. I was seven, he was nine. He was the neighborhood bully, and he always used to thump me on the back or stick his bubble gum in my hair. He trapped me in the park one day when I was in the sandbox. He jumped on top of me and pinned my arms down with his legs and laughed in my face. He then would spit slowly, letting it dribble out of his mouth in one long pendulous strand and let it hang over my face, and at the last second he would suck it back up. "Say you're a pussy, tell me you're a pussy an' I'll let you go," he said. I squeezed my eyes shut, tried to hard not to cry, I would not cry, then he started getting mad. He picked up a blade of grass, held it before my eyes and told me that unless I informed him just how big a pussy I was, he would take the blade of grass, stick up my nose and tickle my brain with it. I struggled in silence and up my nose went the blade of grass. I started to cry. I got one hand free and I grabbed his wrist. I felt his pulse flash blood into mine. Then it happened. I looked up into his face and I saw his entire life mapped out before me. I saw his birth, I saw his first words and his first steps. I saw all the little frogs and birds he's tortured in his back yard, I saw the smokes he stole from his mom. I saw the girl with braces he would impregnate, marry and abuse. I saw the dead-end job he'd have and the in-laws he hated. I saw the barmaids he would screw around with and all the Budweiser's and boilermakers he would drink. I saw his son on a tricycle that he would ignore and later lose. I saw the day he would put the working end of a shotgun into his mouth and take his own life, I saw it, saw it as if I were there. I knew he would die at thirty-nine, and I stopped crying. He looked at me as if he knew, and he hit me twice in the face until I bled and then ran away. He stared at me from the other side of the park and I looked over and said "You're a pussy," and then he ran home. He never bothered me again. I went home with blood on my face and shirt, but no one noticed, my mother slept the Valium sleep and my father watched TV with the King of Beers, so it was just me in my room looking in my mirror with my bloody face and it was then, in that mirror, that I first saw the bleeding bodies on the wall. As I closed my eyes an angel child whispered an obscenity into my ear and then I did start to cry, really really cry. I cried tears of blood. That was my first time.

Dramatic
Tim, twenties

Tim is an actor in a production of Waiting for Godot, where the director has taken extreme liberties with the script, having the main characters be young dudes in their underwear instead of old men. A representative from the Beckett estate crashes a rehearsal to investigate. She and the director go off to confer, and the other actors follow to eavesdrop, leaving Tim alone with Kevin, who is playing Lucky in the show.

TIM: I mean, on one hand I agree that Theatre is a living and breathing event and that we can only truly communicate with an audience who is on the same emotional level as us, and if that means updating the music or changing the costumes to be more viscerally effective, then that's a good thing, but on the other hand if a playwright wrote something one way it's important to keep it the way it is, even if in doing so the play becomes a dusty museum piece that can be appreciated but not truly experienced. "Theatre is Life, Film is Art, Television is Furniture." I used to have a t-shirt that said that. But now these days the well-told storytelling artistic stuff that used to go to film is moving to television or Netflix, and movies are just becoming a superhero tentpole cartoon circus. And then where does that leave Theatre? Where does that leave Life? Things that were shocking only ten years ago are now commonplace. Movies that appalled people decades ago are now old hat. The surprises are boring, but should we go in and edit them to be more so? We can't with film (unless you're George Lucas), but we can with plays. A film is a record of what happened, while a play happens, is happening, right in front of you. That's the difference, that's the magic. *Avenue Q* updated some things to keep up-to-date, but Gary Coleman's still a character in that show even though he's dead in real life. I guess it comes down to what the playwright would want—do we honor his words or his intent? And if the latter, how can we know his intent? Especially if he's dead. And is it better to have an updated but crucially changed production than no production at all? Should we just let an out-of-date play die? What do you think?

Dramatic
Doug, thirties

Doug is the director of a production of Waiting for Godot, where he has cast the leads as young men in their underwear. He defends his reasons for changing the play to a representative from the Beckett estate.

DOUG: These are modern times; that which was once interesting needs more interest for today's audiences. Most of Shakespeare isn't funny anymore; elitists are the only ones who really enjoy Shakespeare these days, because they can pat themselves on the back for getting the obscure jokes. But there are no belly laughs. There's nothing funny about *A Midsummer Night's Dream*, it's basically a Practical Joke involving Bestiality, Donkey Dicks, and Date Rape with a bunch of gags about how stupid poor people are. And don't get me started on Shakespeare's clowns. Poor actors have to add all kinds of business and hand gestures to even get the concept of what they're saying across using these archaic terms, let alone trying to be funny with them. I've never seen a funny clown in Shakespeare. Oh sure, people say that Shakespeare's comedy "translates well" when it really doesn't. They just want to feel smart and let the other audience members know they're smarter than they are. Of course, in actuality, like everyone else, they're trying hard as fuck to even understand what's going on in front of them. Sure there are a few scenes that are still accidentally funny—Dogberry, the Mechanicals; they get the big larfs because we've just watched some impenetrable romance or whatever go on and we're just dying out there. "They say it's a comedy, there must be something to laugh at, I paid for this culture, I'd better get my money's worth. HA HA HA" It's bullshit. People say Shakespeare is funny. He's not. Not anymore. And neither is Beckett. His textual allusions are slowly falling by the wayside for modern Americans, no one knows what a Kapp & Petersen is anymore, no one except pedantic scholars will be understanding the reference to St. Augustine these days: "Do not despair; one of the thieves was saved. Do not presume; one of the thieves was damned"; Pozzo calls his watch a . . . what is it? "A genuine half-hunter, gentlemen, with deadbeat escapement!" I mean, no one knows what the fuck that means, but of course we can't do anything about the text, so we make it an iPhone. Any technobabble is as good as any other. A play should be immediately understood, when you're reading you can go back a page, but not with a play: it just keeps going. For those who haven't studied the play, for those who don't want to treat an entertaining night out as homework, to treat classic theatre as vegetables that we're being forced to eat by an unkind mother . . . We update. We clarify. To be effective, we must substitute what the writer couldn't have foreseen for what we know now.

Comic
Grayson, early twenties

Sam Grayson is in his early 20's, attending a job interview. It appears there is a problem with his urine test.

GRAYSON: Listen . . . I was . . .

(He leans in closer.)

I was at a party two weeks ago. I'm not a party animal, I swear. I just . . . Well . . . things got out of hand. And I . . . Well, I may have tried marijuana. But it was just one drag, I swear, and I've never done it before and it'll never happen again. I promise. *(pause)* My buddies told me not to worry, that it would all wear off before the test, but . . . I . . . I've been stressing out about this all week. I really want this job, Mr. Gibbons. I've always wanted to be a telemarketer. Even when I was a child, I would call up the Cookie Monster hotline and try to sell him Oreos. He was my biggest customer. I sold a bag of garbage once to Oscar the Grouch. Invisible ink to Snuffleupagus. And I . . . Well, I promise you, Mr. Gibbons, if you give me a second chance, I will never let you down again. I will take a drug test every day from now until I retire. Or . . . until you downsize and let me go. Just . . . I'll be the best salesman you ever had. I promise. It was a stupid party and a very bad idea. I was irresponsible, and I'm . . . really very sorry. Please give me another chance.

Dramatic
Billy, twenty-one

The Wakeville Cemetery, 1945. Billy, a WWII vet breaks up with an old girlfriend, Six, to marry another, Tweedy.

BILLY: You just don't get it, Six. I had to stop writing you. Not you and Tweed. You. I couldn't make up things for you anymore. And I knew I couldn't tell you the truth. I wrote Tweed and told her not to tell you. I wished it could have been different. I wished it up to the day I stopped writing you. But you run out of wishes real fast over there. You filled your letters with so many dreams and so much hope, you scared the shit out of me. I'm sorry. I kept all your letters. And I'll read all of them someday. You need somebody you can dream with. You need somebody to give you a whole basketful of dreams. All I seem to be able to do is to play in the dirt 'til it gets dark, have some supper and go to bed. I gotta be alone! I'm marrying Tweedy so I *can* be alone. You understand me? You're just like all the rest. You, my Ma, Aunt Edie, the neighbors—you all want to get inside me. You all think you can take away what's goin' on in here! But you can't! Nobody can. And when you try, all you do is eat me up a little more. You let others inside you—and all they do is go and die right in front of you and take part of you with them. You all take so much sometimes I don't even know if *I'm* still here. Well, Tweed ain't like that. She's not taking anything! I love her . . . I love her 'cause I don't have to go through any of this with her. We don't even have to talk. Don't you understand, I've got nothing to give right now- to anybody. But that doesn't matter to her. Look, Six, I gotta go. We gotta drive back.

She didn't even want to bring me here. This just ain't a peaceful place for everybody. Makes me feel like a . . . I don't know if I'll be back. Tweed'll call you about the wedding and all. You take care of yourself.

Dramatic
A, thirties

Believing his wife and best friend are having an affair, "A" has a mental breakdown during a pitch meeting with television executives.

A: I'm going to write the first television drama in history . . . with absolutely *no conflict.* None. Zero. I'm thinking kind of a kaleidoscope-mosaic-thing: There's this family. And they really love each other. And things are going pretty well for them. We watch them eat breakfast, and breakfast is delicious. They go off to work and school, and it's all pretty rewarding. And then they all come home and tell each other about it. And when one of them talks, the rest of them really listen, they really care what that person has to say. At night, they go to sleep, and dream sweet dreams. It's also about this young couple. And they're really in love. And we just sort of . . . *follow them around while they do things together:* Go to the movies, go for walks, kiss, make love, talk about the future. And we can see that they're really good for each other. We can tell that they're gonna make it. It's also about this guy who loves his job. But he's not a workaholic; he's got a good balance going. It's a rewarding job, but it allows him to be creative without devouring him whole. Imagine that. *Imagine that if you are capable.* And on the weekends, get this: *He goes to the cottage with his dog.* He sits on the dock, throws sticks in the water, and nurses an ice-cold bottle of beer. Never more than three. He is sublimely happy. We want to know these people. We want to *be* these people. Because they are happy. We don't want anything bad to ever happen to them, and the beautiful thing is, we know that nothing ever will. And that's why we'll keep tuning in. Because we'll know that once every week, if only for an hour, we don't have to worry. Everything will be taken care of. Everyone will be safe. It's so simple and perfect, I don't know why no one's ever thought of it before. I can see by your faces that you all think I've lost it—I haven't. *I am just so tired of shilling bullshit.* Look, we all know that I could have sold you this regurgitated cop-show dreck if I'd really wanted to. I've done it before. I'm good at it. If I'd wanted to, I bet I could have convinced a hell of a lot of you that this terrible, *terrible* idea would make a really neat TV show. Most of you, anyway. Some of you.

For information on this author, click on the WRITERS tab at www.smithandkraus.com.

Dramatic
C, thirties

*A past-his-prime almost-but-never-was film actor,
"C" has his first theatre audition in years with this
confessional piece, which also happens to parallel
his own personal life.*

C: I'm sorry. Forgive me. Forgive me, for I have sinned. This
is my first and last confession. (*Silence*) I have had
impure thoughts. I have been irresponsible. I have been
young and stupid. I have been old and set in my ways. I
have not accepted God into my heart. Which . . . makes
this whole thing a bit problematic. I have taken God's
name in vain, both casually and with complete convic-
tion. I have had gods before God, and grown up trying
to emulate them. I have made of myself an idol, to be
worshipped. I have made a willow cabin at your gate. I
have been lustful. Gluttonous. Greedy. Lazy. Vengeful.
Jealous. And proud. I have committed adultery. Almost
to memory. I have coveted my neighbor's wife. Repeat-
edly. I have stolen, and called it mine. I have lied, and
made a decent living at it. I have killed, and been praised
for it. I have eaten red meat on Friday, and enjoyed it. I
have worked on Sunday, and received overtime for it. I
have dishonored my mother and father, and rarely visit or
send cards. I have been restless. I have wandered. I have
been a good thief. I have been the bad son. I have eaten
from the bad apple, and so become one. I have murdered
my brother. I have hated. I have loved. I have lied about
loving. I have hated the one that I loved. I have received
love and not given it. I have given love and not received
it. I have made love while thinking of another. I have

said "I love you" while thinking of another. I have had doubts. I have been distracted. I have been thoughtless. I have been selfish. I have thought mainly about myself. I have wished harm. I have inflicted harm. I have tried to be happy. I have done this. I have done all of this. And I am not sorry. Please. Forgive me. Please. I want love. I want only love. (*Silence*) Are you there? Are you even there?

For information on this author, click on the WRITERS tab at www.smithandkraus.com.

Dramatic
Max, thirties

Max has schizoid personality disorder and is participating in a clinical trial of new drugs to cure it. He describes an event which happened in his fantasy world to Whitney, another participant in the study.

MAX: There was a woman. In the hole. I'd seen her briefly in the drug store. She was ahead of me in line with her two daughters. One named Andrea. She called her by name. And I noticed that she was nice with her daughters. Charming. That's all. Then the next morning, I woke up and the lady from the infomercials about the George Foreman grill, who had been in the hole for about three weeks, was gone. Dead. And this woman, Andrea's mother, I never knew her name, was in her place. And I thought, okay, great, here we go again. But from the start, this woman, Andrea's mother, was different. She never panicked. She hid her fear behind convincing bravado. She kept her humor. She tried to talk to whoever is behind the door and I think whoever it is . . . liked her. She was brave. She never gave up hope. She set up an exercise and meditation routine. She had this amazing spirit. And she survived. Before Andrea's mother the longest a woman had lasted in the hole was three months. More usually they stayed around six weeks. But Andrea's mother was in the hole for two years and eight months. I don't know why she survived so long. But she did. And every morning I would wake up and be terrified to look in the hole. Because I didn't want her to be gone—be dead—after she had lasted so long and tried so hard and kept her little girls so foremost in her mind. She estimated when their birthdays happened and celebrated.

And she started to talk to herself and I learned so much about her. She gave me hope. That he might stop. That if she were gone one day, I might wake up and the door to the hole might be open and the hole might be empty. With police tape stretched across the door. And I would know she got out. She got saved. But after two years of living with her always with me—in the hole inside me—I started to get this awful sense that the killer was getting the itch again. That she was increasingly in danger. I started to wake up crying each morning because I expected her to be gone. And so I stopped sleeping. I thought if I didn't go to sleep he couldn't sneak her out of the hole. He couldn't come in and take her if I was watching, so I kept vigil. For Andrea's mother. To keep her safe. I paced and scratched myself with safety pins to stay awake, until my arms were covered with scabs. And I squeezed lemon juice into my eyes to keep them open. And I stayed awake for about ten days. In the time I spent awake, pacing in my apartment, over the course of those ten days, she finally broke. She broke completely five days into my vigil and she cried and pleaded like she had never cried or pleaded before. She called out for her little girls. She called out for her mother. And after the sixth day, she started calling out . . . for me. . . . . *Max. Help me. I know you're watching.* She knew my name. Somehow. In her panic. She called my name. Over and over. And I stayed awake for her as long as I could. And I kept her safe. Then my uncle came to my apartment. I hadn't been to work or returned any calls. And he came in and saw me. And they put me in the hospital, and they sedated me. It took four times the normal dose to put me under. Because I didn't want to lose her.

Dramatic
Mac, thirty-four

Mac is a childhood friend of Mae's sister Hannah (who he's had a crush on since the 4th grade). But here he is – over 20 years later – in Mae's childhood bedroom about to hook up with Mae. Mae's living at home because her dad has a rare, aggressive form of cancer. And Mac wants nothing more than to connect with Mae and make her feel less alone.

MAC: You know, I've been thinking about you. I've been thinking about you because . . . My mom, when she had me, was just 19. And when kids used to make fun of me at school and stuff and be mean to me, I used to say: If everyone lives to 100. And my mom is 26 and *your m*om is 44 or whatever, then that means that I get 18 more years with my mom than you do. But I mean, of course, that's not true. Because my mom could die before your dad, I mean, still. Even with everything. It's possible. Like my mom lives in California and I see her like once maybe twice a year if I'm lucky for a few days at a time. And you've been here for what? Six weeks? So that's like six years in my book. And even if I added up all the days all the days I'm going to spend with my mom for the rest of my life, so let's say, one week a year times 50 more years that's like 50 weeks that's like one more year of life, one more year of actual days, spent together, in each other's company, I mean, after 18 years of growing up together, one more year of days, and I know there's like the Internet and phone calls and stuff, but one more year of *actual days together* in each other's company before . . . Sorry. Maybe I should shut up.

THE ART OF BAD MEN © 2014 by Vincent Delaney. Reprinted by permission of Mark Orsini, Bret Adams Ltd. For performance rights, contact Mark Orsini. (morsini@bretadamsltd.net)

BECAUSE ME © 2015 by Max Baker. Reprinted by permission of Trice Koopman, Koopman Management. For performance rights, contact Trice Koopman (tk@koopmanmgmt.com)

BREACH © 2014 by Tom Baum. Reprinted by permission of Tom Baum. For performance rights, contact Tom Baum (tombaum@gmail.com)

BROKEN © 2015 by David Meyers. Reprinted by permission of Elaine Devlin, Elaine Devlin Literary, Inc. For performance rights, contact Elaine Devlin (edevlinlit@aol.com)

CHARLES FRANCIS CHAN JR.'S EXOTIC ORIENTAL MURDER MYSTERY © 2015 by Lloyd Suh. Reprinted by permission of Beth Blickers, Agency for the Performing Arts. For performance rights, contact Beth Blickers (bblickers@apa-agency.com)

CLOSURE © 2015 by Richard Dresser. Reprinted by permission of Jessica Amato, The Gersh Agenc. For performance rights, contact Jessica Amato. (jamato@gershny.com)

CONSIDER THE FICUS © 2015 by Audrey Cefaly. Reprinted by permission of Audrey Cafaly. For performance rights, contact Audrey Cafaly. (alcefaly@gmail.com)

COMPOSURE © 2015 by Scott Sickles. Reprinted by permission of Barbara Hogenson, Barbara Hogenson Agency. For performance rights, contact Barbara Hogenson. (bhogenson@aol.com)

THE CUBAN SPRING © 2013 by Vanessa Garcia. Reprinted by permission of Vanessa Garcia. For performance rights, contact Vanessa Garcia. (vgarcia43@yahoo.com)

CURSE OF THE WOLF MAN © 2015 by CURSE OF THE WOLF MAN. Reprinted by permission of Don Nigro. For performance rights, contact Samuel French, Inc., 212-206-8990, www.samuelfrench.com

DIDO OF IDAHO © 2015 by Abby Rosebrock. Reprinted by permission of Abby Rosebrosk. For performance rights, contact Abby Rosebrosk (m.abigail.rosebrock@gmail.com)

DOSTOYEVSKI © 2015 by Don Nigro. Reprinted by permission of Don Nigro. For performance rights, contact Samuel French, Inc., 212-206-8990, (www.samuelfrench.com)

DREAM OF A DEER AT DUSK © 2014 by Adam Kraar. Reprinted by permission of Elaine Devlin, Elaine Devlin Literary, Inc. For performance rights, contact Elaine Devlin. (edevlinlit@aol.com)

EVERYTHING'S FREE! © 2015 by Sam Graber. Reprinted by permission of Sam Graber. For performance rights, contact Sam Graber (samgraber@comcast.net)

EYES SHUT. DOOR OPEN © 2015 by Cassie M. Seinuk. Reprinted by permission of Cassie M. Seinuk. For performance rights, contact Cassie M. Seinuk. (cmseinuk@gmail.com)

FAITH © 2015 by James McLindon. Reprinted by permission of James McLindon. For performance rights, contact James McLindon (jmclindon@gmail.com)

THE FEAST © 2015 by Celine Song. Reprinted by permission of Celine Song. For performance rights, contact Celine Song. (song.celine@gmail.com)

FIVE TIMES IN ONE NIGHT © 2016 by Chiara Atik. Reprinted by permission of Chiara Atik. For performance rights, contact Derek Zasky, William Morris Endeavor (dsz@wmeentertaiment.com)

FOR THE LOYAL © 2015 by Lee Blessing. Reprinted by permission of Lee Blessing. For performance rights, contact Dramatists Play Service, 440 Park Ave. S., New York, NY 10016 (www.dramatists.com) (212-683-8960).

THE GHOSTS OF US © 2016 by Rebecca Gorman O'Neill. Reprinted by permission of Rebecca Gorman O'Neill. For performance rights, contact Rebecca Gorman O'Neill (gormanreb@aol.com)

THE GODDESS OF MURDEROUS RAIN © 2015 by Don Nigro. Reprinted by permission of Don Nigro. For performance rights, contact Samuel French, Inc., 212-206-8990, www.samuelfrench.com

THE GRASS IS GREENEST AT THE HOUSTON ASTRODOME © 2014 by Michael Ross Albert. Reprinted by permission of Michael Ross Albert. For performance rights, contact Michael Ross Albert. (info@michaelrossalbert.com)

GRAVEYARD OF EMPIRES © 2015 by Elaine Romero. Reprinted by permission of Bruce Ostler, Bret Adams Ltd. For performance rights, contact Bruce Ostler.

(bostler@bretadamsltd.net)

THE HEAD HUNTER © 2000 by Mark Borkowski. Reprinted by permission of Marta Praeger, Robert H. Freedman Dramatic Agency. For performance rights, contact Marta Praeger. (mp@bromasite.com)

HER BROTHER'S KEEPER © 2015 by Laura Hirschberg. Reprinted by permission of Laura Hirschberg. For performance rights, contact Laura Hirschberg (laura.hirschberg@gmail.com)

HOW TO GET INTO BUILDINGS © 2012 by Trish Harnetiaux. Reprinted by permission of Bailey Williams, AO International. For performance rights, contact Bailey Williams (bwilliams@aoegelinternational.com)

I AM NOT AN ALLEGORY © 2015 by Libby Emmons. Reprinted by permission of Libby Emmons. For performance rights, contact Libby Emmons (li88yemmons@gmail.com)

I COULD NEVER LIVE HERE © 2015 by C.S. Hanson. Reprinted by permission of C.S. Hanson. For performance rights, contact C.S. Hanson (cshansonplays@yahoo.com)

I LOVE YOU, MAN © 2015 by Audrey Cefaly. Reprinted by permission of Audrey Cafaly. For performance rights, contact Audrey Cafaly (alcefaly@gmail.com)

JAMES DEAN AND THE DEVIL © 2016 by Rosary Hartel O'Neill. Reprinted by permission of Rosary Hartel O'Neill. For performance rights, contact Rosary Hartel O'Neill. (rosaryo@aol.com)

KENTUCKY © 2015 by Leah Tanako Winkler. Reprinted by permission of Leah Tanako Wiinkler. For performance rights, contact Leah Tanako Wiinkler (leahnana@gmail.com)

KISSED THE GIRLS AND MADE THEM CRY © 2015 by Arlene Hutton. Reprinted by permission of Pat McLaughlin, Beacon Artists Agency. For performance rights, contact Pat McLaughlin (beaconagency@hotmail.com)

L.A.DELI © 2014 by Sam Bobrick. Reprinted by permission of Ron Gwiazda, Abrams Artists. For performance rights, contact Ron Gwiazda. (ron.gwiazda@abramsartny.com)

LE SWITCH © 2015 by Philip Dawkins. Reprinted by permission of Beth Blickers, Agency for the Performing Arts. For performance rights, contact Beth Blickers (bblickers@apa-agency.com)

LEVELING UP © 2014 by Deborah Zoe Laufer. Reprinted by permission of Deborah Zoe Laufer. For performance rights, contact Deborah Zoe Laufer. (dzlaufer@optimum.net)

LIGHTS RISE ON GRACE © 2015 by Chad Beckim. Reprinted by permission of Chad Beckim. For performance rights, contact Chad Beckim (chadbeckim1@yahoo.com)

THE LORELEI © 2015 by Don Nigro. Reprinted by permission of Don Nigro. For performance rights, contact Samuel French, Inc., 212-206-8990, www.samuelfrench.com

LOTTERY PLAY © 2015 by Sam Graber. Reprinted by permission of Sam Graber. For performance rights, contact

Sam Graber (samgraber@comcast.net)

LUNCH WITH MRS. BASKIN © 2014 by Sam Bobrick. Reprinted by permission of Ron Gwiazda, Abrams Artists. For performance rights, contact Ron Gwiazda (ron. gwiazda@abramsartny.com)

MUTT © 2014 by Christopher Chenn. Reprinted by permission of Bailey Williams, AO International. For performance rights, contact Bailey Williams (bwilliams@ aoegelinternational.com)

NEED TO KNOW © 2016 by Jonathan Caren. Reprinted by permission of Jared Weber, ICM Partners. For performance rights, contact Di Glazer, ICM Partners (dglazer@ icmpartners.com)

NEW COUNTRY © 2015 by Mark Roberts. Reprinted by permission of Bailey Williams, AO International. For performance rights, contact Dramatists Play Service, 440 Park Ave. S., New York, NY 10016 (www.dramatists. com) (212-683-8960).

NIGHT OF THE LIVING DEAD © 2015 by Ron Riekki. Reprinted by permission of Ron Riekki. For performance rights, contact Ron Riekki (ronriekki@hotmail.com)

ONE IN THE CHAMBER © 2014 by Marja-Lewis Ryan. Reprinted by permission of Rachel Viola, United Talent Agency. For performance rights, contact Rachel Viola. (violar@unitedtalent.com)

THE OTHER THING © 2015 by Emily Schwend. Reprinted by permission of Leah Hamos, Gersh Agency. For performance rights, contact Leah Hamos. (lhamos@ gershny.com)

PARIS AT DAWN © 2016 by Eric Grant. Reprinted by permission of Eric Grant. For performance rights, contact Eric Grant. (egrant94@gmail.com)

A PLACE THAT LOOKS LIKE DAVENPORT © 2015 by Paul Lewis. Reprinted by permission of Paul Lewis.